NONE BUT THE VALIANT

Robert Hayhoo

l DL

Also available in the Target Adventure Series:

True Life

WINGS OF GLORY—Graeme Cook
an action-packed history of aerial warfare

Fiction

DOCTOR WHO AND THE DALEKS

DOCTOR WHO AND THE ZARBI

DOCTOR WHO AND THE CRUSADERS

THE NIGHTMARE RALLY

A TARGET ADVENTURE

NONE BUT THE VALIANT

True stories of war at sea

GRAEME COOK

TARGET

a division of

Universal-Tandem Publishing Co., Ltd.
14 Gloucester Road, London SW7 4RD

First published in Great Britain by Rupert Hart-Davis, Ltd., 1972

First published in this edition by
Universal-Tandem Publishing Co., Ltd., 1973

ISBN 0 426 10276 2

Copyright © Graeme Cook, 1972

Printed in Great Britain by The Anchor Press Ltd.,
and bound by Wm. Brendon & Son Ltd., both of Tiptree, Essex

To Sheila, my wife

Acknowledgements

The author wishes to express his sincere gratitude to Captain Günther Raeder, Naval Attaché to the Federal German Embassy, London, for his enthusiastic co-operation in gathering much of the background information contained in this book.

Thanks are also due to Mr J. T. Waldron, Mr J. Gleeson and their publishers, Evans Brothers Limited, for their kind permission to use certain of the facts contained in a highly-readable book, *The Frogmen*.

My special thanks go to Valerie Furniss who painstakingly typed my entire manuscript and to the Director and staff of the Imperial War Museum, London, for their valuable assistance with my research.

G.C.

Contents

List of Illustrations

(All photographs reproduced by kind permission of the
Director, Imperial War Museum, London.)

Foreword

The outbreak of the First World War brought with it a highly-sophisticated and mechanised form of naval warfare; one in which stealth and cunning of submarine commanders and the dash of the fast destroyers, as well as the massed fire-power of colossal super-dreadnoughts, were to play a decisive part. But however different the vessels were from those which had done battle in previous wars, the courage and fortitude of the men who sailed in them remained unchanged. The advance in technology altered the strategy of modern naval warfare but the ultimate success or failure of naval operations depended almost entirely upon the men who served in these ships. This book tells the story of some of these gallant sailors and the battles in which they fought during two world wars.

Submarine Patrol

The long, slim bow of HM Submarine E-11 cut its way through the dark waves as it nosed towards the mouth of the Dardanelles, the narrow stretch of water flowing between the Aegean and Black Seas, separating Europe and Asia. In the conning tower, which jutted like a slender finger out of the bubbling seas, stood Lieutenant Commander Martin Nasmyth VC, his eyes intent on the yawning gap in the land in front of him.

It was 5 August 1915, and Europe was the setting for the bloodiest conflict in the history of mankind, the First World War. On land, the armies of the Central Powers and the Allies were locked in fierce combat, with both sides suffering the most unbelievable losses merely to advance in many cases only a few yards. Thousands of men perished by the hour in the wholesale slaughter amid the mud-filled trenches and the deep holes gouged in the earth by exploding shells, while at sea the British Fleet ruled the waves.

Turkey was among those countries which sided with Germany's Kaiser against Britain and her allies and it was inevitable therefore that the Dardanelles and the Sea of Marmora, across which the Turks' war supplies flowed, should be the scene of some bitter fighting.

The long narrow straits known as the Dardanelles

were the only sea-link with the Black Sea and if the Allies were to crush the Turks they had first to sever that supply line. This, as they were soon to discover, was to be no easy task even for the invincible British Fleet. The shores of the Dardanelles stretching some forty miles were lined with more than a hundred guns of assorted types, which covered every inch of the Straits. In addition there were clusters of torpedo tubes at strategic points and, by night, the waters were ablaze with light as searchlight batteries continually swept the area. But if that were not enough, parts of the sea-passage were heavily mined against surface ships and at the narrowest point, an anti-submarine net was stretched from one shore to the other.

In March 1915, a fleet of British and French ships had tried to run the gaunlet of the Turkish guns and been driven back under a furious barrage of fire with the loss of four ships. It seemed that there was to be no way of mounting a sea-borne attack which would silence these guns and give the British Fleet access to the Black Sea, and at the same time help them sever the supply-link. Then a plan was conceived to land an Allied Army and attack the guns from behind, and so it was that in April 1915 troops fought their way ashore at a rocky peninsula called Gallipoli to begin a campaign which was to be nothing short of disaster, and cost the lives of thousands of men. While these gallant soldiers met the wrath of the Turkish fire power, reinforcements for the defending army were pouring across the Sea of Marmora to come to the aid of their comrades and try to push the Allied forces back in the sea. The ensuing clash of determined men resulted in a long, drawn out war of slaughter lasting for several months during which neither side seemed to gain any advantage.

The chances of the Allies turning this conflict into a victory were hopeless while the Turks continued to be fed with men and supplies across the Marmora, and it was to stem the tide of reinforcements that the Admiralty sent submarines through the Dardanelles in the hope that they could sink the transport ships that were ferrying the troops and supplies across the Turkish-held lake of Marmora.

The submarines, however, found the passage almost impossible under the weight of the Turkish defences, and the first four to attempt the voyage were all sunk or destroyed. The fifth, however, HMS E-14, under the command of Lieutenant Commander Edward Boyle RN, succeeded and after an epic foray in the Marmora, during which she sank a ship carrying 6,000 enemy troops, she escaped and Boyle was awarded the Victoria Cross for his daring exploit.

The next submarine to successfully reach the Marmora was the E-11, captained by Lieutenant Commander Nasmyth who, during his twenty-day stay in the Marmora, sank four transports and a gun-boat as well as setting on fire twelve sailing dhows which were transporting war cargoes. Not content with that, Nasmyth sneaked into the harbour at Constantinople and torpedoed an ammunition ship. He, like Boyle, was awarded the Victoria Cross for his courageous patrol in the Marmora. It was nothing short of amazing that Nasmyth succeeded in his mission considering the opposition he had to face, not to mention the loss of a periscope which was holed by a Turkish shell. Skill and a certain amount of luck had brought Nasmyth and his crew safely back from the Marmora, and one would have thought it suicidal for him to have tried again, but Nasmyth was determined, and so it was that on the black August night he found himself once more embarking on an epic adventure . . .

Ahead of him, with the submarine's diesel engines making what seemed like a terrible din and one that would certainly betray their presence to the Turks on shore, Nasmyth could see the searchlights sweeping the water, constantly on the look-out for Allied ships that might try to slip in at night. Nasmyth could not negotiate the channel of water submerged because he would have to surface at some point and recharge his batteries while he sat motionless in the water, unable to crash-dive if he were spotted by the enemy. His only hope of penetrating the Dardanelles was to remain on the surface, running on his diesels, and hope that he would not be spotted. If he were, then he would at least be able to crash-dive and try to avoid the enemy guns. So it was that E-11 slid on into the mouth of the Dardanelles, her bows cutting through the water sending the waves rolling along her casing in sweeping undulation before casting up a phosphorescent wake behind the submarine.

Tension mounted as the submarine edged between the gaping jaws of the Dardanelles. The searchlights were but a few hundred yards away and the thin fingers of light crept across the waves. At any moment E-11 could be bathed in light and the guns would open up, hurtling shells at the sub. Everything on board was ready for a crash-dive should the order be given. Nasmyth's hands gripped the rim of the conning tower as he stood on the bridge tensely watching the pools of light as they played over the water, waiting for the moment when one of those white circles would settle on his boat. But miraculously, although the sub was for one fleeting moment partially illuminated, she succeeded in creeping past the first battery of searchlights undiscovered.

Nasmyth had no reason to feel relieved, though, for there was worse to come. Even without the searchlights to light up the water, keen eyes still peered out over the Straits from the gun emplacements along the shore. He knew that his next major obstacle would be the minefield and to penetrate this he would have to dive. When he had last made this voyage he discovered that the Turks had anchored their mines as defence against surface ships. Nasmyth was able to slip through the minefield by diving deep and avoided the lethal prongs on the highly-explosive spheres that bobbed about on the surface and a few feet under it.

Just after 4 o'clock on the morning of the 6th, Nasmyth gave the order to dive and the boat slid beneath the waves under battery power. Only occasionally did he take E-11 to periscope depth to check his bearings.

With a few minutes to go before entering the minefield things started to go wrong and the boat suddenly began to slow down as if something were trying to pull her back. The deck suddenly tilted crazily as the bows were forced upwards. What had happened, although Nasmyth was not to discover this until later, was that the Turks had strung a steel hawser across the channel just below the surface of the water. The idea was that it would foul the periscopes of enemy submarines by bending them backwards. E-11 had got caught up in the wire and the forward motion of the boat was forcing the bows upwards, exposing them to any watchful gunner on the shore. Luckily, though, they were not spotted and Nasmyth dived deep, wriggling free of the wires as he did so. But one horrifying thought plagued his mind as E-11 slid away from the wire. Had the periscope been broken? If so they would be useless as a fighting ship in the

Marmora—if they ever got there. With their 'scope wrecked they would be without eyes to make their underwater attacks. Gingerly, Nasmyth edged the boat up to the surface and scrambled on to the conning tower to inspect the damage. But he heaved a sigh of relief when he discovered that the 'scope was undamaged and E-11 dived once more, this time to sixty feet, well out of the way of wire hawsers. In just a few minutes he would be into the minefield.

Inside the submarine all was quiet save for the dull hum of the motors, and only those who had to were working, guiding the boat through the deep. The others sat motionless, trying to visualise the long mine cables anchored to the sea-bed resembling a forest of slender trees through which they were sailing. Then it happened. Suddenly there was an ear-piercing screech as an anchor cable dragged along the side of the boat from stem to stern. There was, however, no cause to worry as the mines themselves, the explosive orbs at the ends of the cables, were far above them. Again and again it came, that loud rasping sound as the cables scraped along the outer casing of the submarine.

After a few moments all was quiet. Everyone listened intently, hardly daring to breathe. Then came the sound they had all been dreading and one that very few submariners live to hear twice. With an almighty *clang* that reverberated through the ship the metal orb of a mine hit the boat's side. Death could be only a fraction of a second away when one of these deadly prongs touched the boat. No one was able to speak as their hearts raced in dreadful expectancy. Outside the boat, the mine wavered on the end of its cable, swinging once more towards the boat as it slid forward. In these tension-charged seconds the crew waited with the blood pounding through their veins. They could not get off with it a second time and there was nothing they could do to steer the ship away from the mine. Then, like the crash of thunder, it came . . . *clang!* Their guardian angel must have been watching over them for there was no explosion and the submarine slipped away from the mine. Nasmyth and his crew could hardly believe their good fortune. They had brushed sides with death and escaped. Perhaps this was a good omen for their patrol.

Nasmyth figured that the submarine must have hit the mine on its underpart where there were no prongs to detonate it. That and luck had saved them from disaster. Nasmyth dived deeper with mine anchor chains scraping along the casing as he went, then he levelled off at eighty feet and felt his way deeper into the Dardanelles. The next barrier in his path was the anti-submarine net, stretched across the narrows and descending right to the sea-bed. Minutes later the submarine charged into the net which cast the boat upwards, throwing the crew off balance. When the submarine finally came to a halt, she was entangled in the net and Nasmyth decided that there was but one way through it. He ordered full ahead and the motors whined at full pitch, thrusting the submarine deeper into the net, struggling to get through. Then as if in a gasp, the wires parted and the submarine shot forward, clear through the net. They were through. The last obstacle in their path had been passed. Now they had to negotiate the remaining miles of the Straits before getting down to the job they had been sent to do and Nasmyth, after they had gone some little way, brought the submarine to periscope depth.

'Up 'scope!' he ordered.

The periscope rose from its well and he clutched the handles, tense with expectation at what he would find. With his eyes hard against the rubber protectors on the eye-pieces, he swung the 'scope around in a full 360 degrees. The bay he found himself in was empty of warships but he did, however, sight a target—a transport ship. His eyes gleamed.

'Action stations!' he ordered and the crew scrambled to their battle-positions for the attack.

Methodically, Nasmyth went through the drill for the attack. The nose of the submarine pointed directly at the transport and the commander peered through the 'scope, then ordered the bow tubes to be flooded. In an instant there was the familiar hiss of compressed air as water was forced out of the forward trim tank and into the tubes.

A few moments later Lieutenant D'Oyly Hughes, Nasmyth's 'Number One', reported, 'Bow tubes ready, sir!'

Still Nasmyth peered through the 'scope making absolutely sure that he was on target.

'Stand by port bow tube,' he said hurriedly. Then there was a slight pause, then '. . . FIRE!'

The submarine shuddered as the torpedo shot out of the tube, on course for the transport. Nasmyth watched the trail of bubbles from the torpedo's whirling propeller tracing a line towards the transport, while D'Oyly counted out the seconds.

'Any moment . . . Now!' he shouted.

A split second later there came a muffled bang and through the 'scope Nasmyth saw a great column of water rise amidships on the transport. Almost instantly, the ship keeled over as tons of water rushed into the gash in her side. She was doomed. That, Nasmyth thought, was one ship that wouldn't be taking supplies to the Turks any more. Yells of delight at the success echoed through E-11. Nasmyth had made his first 'kill' of the patrol. It was to be the first of many in an exciting and action-packed mission.

Nasmyth took his boat away from the area in which he had made the attack, knowing full well that the Turks would be out in force looking for the sub that had sunk their transport. Hours later in a boat dense with the stench of human bodies Nasmyth gave the order, 'Prepare to surface!' and the submarine broke water. But no sooner had it done so than a Turkish gun-boat was seen pounding down on them.

'Dive! Dive! Dive!' Nasmyth yelled, and the boat slid towards the watery sanctuary.

Later Nasmyth tried again to reach the surface with the same result. By then the atmosphere in the boat was becoming almost unbearable. They had been submerged for so long that the air had become fouled and the simple act of breathing was becoming more and more difficult. Again he tried and again the gun-boat was too close for safety. Nasmyth had to surface soon or the bad air would begin to have a serious effect on the men in the boat.

At last on the fourth try, he found himself in a deserted sea. The hatches were thrown open and the sweet smell of fresh air reached their nostrils and was inhaled deeply, revitalising weakened bodies. Everyone who could went on deck to revel in the bliss of the sweet-smelling air. But their moment of pleasure was soon to come to an abrupt end as they lay there idly gazing into the bright cloudless sky. No one heard the drone of the aircraft engine but in an instant they all heard the ominous whistle of two bombs as they hurtled down towards them. Seconds later there were two violent explosions as the bombs hit the water alongside the ship thrusting great columns of water into the air. Men leapt from their resting places and dived for the hatches as the emergency crash-dive hooter sounded throughout the ship. With hatches secured, the boat plunged down into the deep, away from the aircraft circling overhead. Miraculously, the boat was undamaged and Nasmyth got underway again. But he knew now that the Turks were going all-out to trace and attack the submarine, and he would have to keep an ever-watchful eye on the sky and the sea. There would be no time to relax during this arduous patrol.

Hours later they nosed into their objective—the Sea of Marmora. At last they had arrived at their destination. Now their job was to seek out targets and destroy them but first Nasmyth had an important appointment to keep. As his submarine chugged through the waves he stood on the conning tower scanning the sea with his binoculars until he saw it—the familiar shape of another submarine ploughing its way through the sea towards him. It was E-14, under the command of Lieutenant Commander Edward Boyle VC, another veteran of the Marmora.

Nasmyth and Boyle greeted each other warmly as their boats drew alongside each other. There was little time to waste on pleasantries, though. With their boats motionless in the water they were both easy targets for enemy aircraft so they got down to the business of exchanging information.

Boyle told Nasmyth that he had found few worthwhile targets in the Marmora and said that the Turks now seemed to be getting most of their supplies through by the road to Gallipoli which skirted the sea. This news gave Nasmyth food for thought. Why not, he pondered, deprive the Turks of their road link as well as hounding them at sea? But his thoughts were cut short when Boyle sighted a gun-boat racing towards them across the sea from the direction of Gallipoli.

Both men acted swiftly agreeing on a hasty attack plan to each other. Nasmyth dived while E-14 remained on the surface to 'lure' the gun-boat into E-11's sights. Staying at periscope depth, Nasmyth peered through his 'scope, watching the gun-boat approach. Then came his order: 'Fire!' and the torpedo lanced through the water and hit the enemy boat, but it did not explode and merely damaged the boat which turned and ran aground on the beach. Nasmyth cursed his luck in having fired what must have been a faulty 'fish'.

It was the following day before the two intrepid submarine commanders got their chance to strike at the enemy once more but this time it was in a particularly unconventional way for a submarine.

During the morning both boats lay off the shore at periscope depth with the two commanders taking occasional peeps at the enemy activity on the road that ran along the shore line. Then Nasmyth noticed a column of troops marching uniformly along the dusty road. Now, he thought, was his chance to catch them on the hop.

With his gun crew waiting, poised for action, beneath the hatches Nasmyth brought the submarine to the surface and before the conning tower was fully exposed above the water, men were pouring out of it and racing for the twelve-pounder gun on deck. In less than a minute, it belched a bright orange flame and a shell raced through the sky and exploded on the road amid the troops. As fast as they could load, Nasmyth's gun crew sent shells hurtling over the shore and into the troops now racing for cover. The bombardment continued until Nasmyth found himself under attack from the shore when the Turks brought up a field gun to retaliate. He had done all he could and decided that the time had come to call off the attack.

That same day the Turkish battleship *Heirreddin Barbarossa* came into Nasmyth's sights and he sent her to the bottom. From then on the patrol was feverish activity almost every minute of the day, with Nasmyth attacking everything that floated, including the Turkish dhows. He had devised a special way of dealing with these boats in order to conserve ammunition. He would surface and order the Turks to abandon ship, then D'Oyly Hughes would go aboard the enemy vessel and set fire to it. There were times when he succeeded in rounding up several of these craft, so Nasmyth lashed them all together and set fire to the lot!

D'Oyly Hughes, Nasmyth's 'Number One', was a burly, twenty-three-year-old Irishman, whose enthusiasm for the fight had continually to be tempered by his captain. He was a man who believed in the bold adventurous approach to the war, and was quite prepared to risk life and limb to get into a scrap with the enemy. His flow of ideas to the captain was never ending and Nasmyth admired him for his untamed enthusiasm, but reluctantly had to turn down most of the Irishman's plans. There was one, however, which caught the captain's imagination . . .

Close to the shore around the Marmora was a railway line which Nasmyth knew carried many of the supplies to Gallipoli. If they could put that track out of action, it would virtually strangle the Turkish forces and cut off their life-line. There was one highly vulnerable spot on that line over a gorge. If that viaduct could be brought down, the line would be well and truly cut so Nasmyth planned to take his submarine into the gorge and bombard the bridge with his twelve-pounder. D'Oyly, however, protested, saying that it was a job for one man who would go ashore and deal with the viaduct, setting explosive charges in the trellis work.

He meant, of course, himself. But Nasmyth was determined to try the bombardment first. That night the submarine crept into the quiet gorge which fortunately contained just enough water for her to remain submerged. Then Nasmyth surfaced and the gun crew dashed to the twelve-pounder and blasted away at the viaduct with shells. For a few minutes there was no reply to the British barrage of fire and the twelve-pounder continued to hurtle shells at the bridge. Several hits were scored but, alas, without much effect. Then suddenly the water around the submarine erupted in great spurts when heavy Turkish guns opened up on the submarine.

As the twelve-pounder seemed to be unable to inflict serious damage on the viaduct which, because of its trellis-work construction, was an extremely difficult target, Nasmyth ordered the gunners off the casing and dived. The submarine slid away out of the gorge with the Turkish shells raining down into the water around it. Once into the open sea and safely out of range of the Turks' guns Nasmyth and D'Oyly reviewed the situation. There was a broad smile on the young Irishman's face when Nasmyth admitted that it seemed like a one-man job after all.

Nasmyth waited until dark that night before taking E-11 into the gorge once more. Moving like phantoms in the night, several men slipped out of the conning tower on to the casing. Among them was D'Oyly, a mountain of a man clad in a swim suit. A few moments later a small raft was slipped into the water followed by D'Oyly himself, who edged into the water behind the raft, and pushed it before him, heading for the dark shore some yards away. On the raft were several bundles, wrapped in waterproof covering, which contained the tools for his expedition that night and included gun-cotton, a pistol with which to light the fuse, a bayonet, a whistle and his uniform. He had been very particular to include his uniform in case of capture as proof that he was not a spy and could not, under the 'rules of war,' be shot.

As D'Oyly scrambled up on to the shore, E-11 slipped away out of the mouth of the gorge to lie in wait for number one to return. D'Oyly hid the raft, then donned his uniform. With his packages under his arms he made his way up the steeply-sloping hillside until he reached the top. Exhausted, but determined to get the job over and done with, he stole into the darkness in search of the railway line.

For a full hour he searched the inky darkness for the line and then he stumbled right into it. Slipping quickly through the night he followed the track until suddenly he stopped dead. He could hear voices ahead of him. Quickly he stowed his explosives at the foot of a tree and crept forward on all fours, gingerly inching his way towards the chattering until he saw them—three Turkish sentries sitting talking, with their rifles stacked beside them. No way through here, he thought, and he set off to make a wide detour, scrambling over low walls, through farmyards and into ditches. Then as he crept slowly through yet another farmyard, the whole world seemed to burst into life around him. He had walked smack into the middle of a chicken run. In an instant chaos reigned as birds fluttered into the air, screeching with alarm. This is it, D'Oyly thought, as he made a run for it and dropped behind a nearby wall. He waited, panting and breathless, for the troops that must come now that the alarm had been given but as the seconds ticked into minutes he realised that no one could have heard the birds, and got underway once more.

At last after a few more tense minutes dashing through the night, he caught sight of the viaduct and immediately any thoughts he had had about planting his explosives on it were shattered. The viaduct was alive with workmen. To make matters even worse, at either end of the viaduct were workmen's fires, presumably lit to give them some source of warmth in the cold night air.

Retracing his steps, but being careful not to stumble into the chicken yard again, D'Oyly made his way back to where he had stowed his explosives and he took them from under the tree. In spite of his set-back he was still determined to damage the line as much as he could, and he found a small culvert which ran through the embankment under the tracks. This, he thought, should do the trick and he set his explosives in the culvert. All that remained now was to ignite the fuse but this had to be done with his pistol, which he knew would alert the Turkish guards who were only some 200 yards away. He had no alternative if his mission was to be a success so he drew his pistol, aimed and fired. The noise echoed out of the culvert like the roar of a cannon and D'Oyly knew that the sentries must be rushing his way to investigate. If they got to the explosive charge before the five minute fuse had burned out they might just be able to save the track from destruction. There seemed only one course open to him . . .

He leapt on to the track and raced headlong down it *towards* the sentries. Moments later he came face to face with them and he levelled his revolver, fired two shots then bolted down the embankment towards the shore amid a hail of bullets from the pursuing Turks. On he charged like a man possessed and slithered down the slope of the hillside. As he dropped earthwards the low rumble of a violent explosion reached his ears. He'd done it. The track was, although he could not see it, ripped up from the ground and bent back in a tangled mass, with the culvert itself a mere heap of rubble. Repair would take weeks and the line was completely out of action.

Reaching the shoreline D'Oyly pulled off his shoes and jacket and leapt into the water. He mustered every ounce of his remaining strength to swim to the safety of the submarine. But as he struggled farther out into the gorge he realised that the submarine was not waiting there for him. He had in fact hit the water some distance away from where he had planned to meet the sub and he knew that he would never be able to swim that distance in his exhausted state, so he headed back for the shore and scrambled on to dry land once more, only to hear the sentries crashing through a patch of wood nearby. Hurriedly he picked himself up and ran along the rocky shore until he saw the all too welcome conning tower of E-11 sticking out of the water. As he plunged into the water and struck out for the sub, Nasmyth spotted him and brought the boat in as near as he could to the shore.

Meanwhile, the sentries opened up with their rifles sending bullets zipping into the water, none of them, luckily, hitting the swimmer. From the deck of the submarine, sailors, armed with rifles, pumped lead towards the shore in a bid to halt the sentries, until at last, D'Oyly's limp and exhausted body was hauled aboard and taken below. With the hatches secure, Nasmyth headed out to sea once more.

D'Oyly's work that night played havoc with the Turkish communications, starving their fighting men of many of the vital supplies they needed to ward off the Allied invasion. He was later decorated with the

Distinguished Service Order in recognition of his courage.

Nasmyth continued his patrol in the Marmora with his score of kills mounting and it was not until 11 September that he was ordered out of the Turkish lake. Once more he braved the Dardanelles and brought his crew safely home to fight another day . . . and fight they did, for E-11 later returned to the Marmora again and remained there for forty-seven days during which time more ships fell victim to her. During her three patrols, Nasmyth and E-11 were responsible for the destruction of no less than one-hundred-and-one enemy vessels. Nasmyth and his fellow submariners had proved beyond doubt that the submarine had revolutionised naval warfare.

The gallant captain of E-11 remained in the Royal Navy to become Admiral Sir Martin Nasmyth VC, a living example of courage to all the men who served under him.

2

The Impostors

Count Felix von Lückner, captain of the windjammer *Seeadler*, peered intently through his binoculars at the British merchant ship as it laboriously cut its way through the rolling Atlantic waves. He watched the merchantman for a few moments longer, examining her closely before taking the binoculars from his eyes. As he did so he grinned slightly, then turned to the helmsman and ordered a change of course to take the *Seeadler* towards the British ship.

The seaman at the helm hauled the huge wheel round in response to his captain's command, and the *Seeadler* lent over as she swept round towards the steamer. Meanwhile on board the merchantman, the British captain watched the windjammer steering towards him and thought how majestic she looked in full sail with her bows dipping and rising in the turbulent seas.

'That's a sight we see too little of these days,' the captain said to his mate, who stood beside him watching *Seeadler* course through the waves.

'She's flying the Norwegian flag, sir,' the mate observed. 'Probably carrying a cargo of timber I shouldn't wonder.' Then he paused. 'Hullo, she's signalling . . . needs help. Wonder what she wants? She doesn't look like she's having trouble.'

The minutes passed until the *Seeadler* was almost alongside the merchantman. From the deck of the windjammer von Lückner shouted through a loud-hailer.

'Ahoy, there! Our chronometer has been playing tricks on us. Can you give me a time check, please?'

'Of course,' yelled the British captain and he reduced speed to keep alongside the *Seeadler* and checked the time, but when he turned round to reply, his mouth dropped open in surprise. The ship's rail on the *Seeadler* was falling away to reveal a heavy gun manned by a gun crew poised, ready to fire point-blank at his ship. The Norwegian flag had been lowered and the German naval ensign run up. An instant later, von Lückner's voice boomed out over the loud-hailer to the unbelieving British crew . . .

'You will prepare to abandon your ship! I am sending over a boarding party. Resistance is useless and no-one will be hurt if you obey my instructions.'

Still somewhat dazed by what had just happened the British captain ordered his men to do as the German had said. He knew only too well that one false move would spell disaster. He was unarmed and completely at the mercy of the German. He had no choice but to surrender his ship.

Von Lückner's boarding party clambered onto the deck of the merchantman and methodically set about looting the ship while the British captain and crew were transferred to the windjammer; then, with their spoils, they returned to the Seeadler.

The British captain had heard many stories of how harshly Allied crews had been treated by their German captors, and it was with some trepidation that he was hauled aboard the German ship. What fate had in store for him he did not know but he prepared himself for the worst. When he straightened himself up after scrambling over the ship's rail, he came face to face with a tall, well-built man with a round open face, dressed in the uniform of a Lieutenant Commander of the German navy.

Von Lückner saluted, then stepped forward and clasped the captain's hand and shook it warmly.

'Welcome aboard the Seeadler, Captain,' he said in as good English as he could muster. 'I regret that our meeting could not have been under happier circumstances. It is, unfortunately, my duty to sink your ship. It is a disagreeable task but, alas, war forces upon us many tasks we do not like to perform. My mate will show you to your quarters, Captain. I know you will not wish to witness the sinking of your ship.'

With that the British captain was shown below where he found to his amazement that comfortable quarters had been prepared for himself and his crew, and a table was being set with a mouth watering meal. For a moment he stood there in disbelief, unable to understand the situation. This couldn't be the German navy he had heard about, he thought. What of all the stories he had heard of brutality to prisoners? It must be some kind of a dream. But he was sharply brought back to reality when the ship shook violently as a gun roared. He dashed to a port-hole to see his ship struck by a shell followed by another and another. Shells ripped into the merchantman's side tearing it open. In a matter of minutes the ship was peppered with holes and thousands of tons of water gushed into the holds and engine room. Fire swept through the ship from stem to stern, and soon she keeled over and sank beneath the waves. Von Lückner's deception had claimed another victim—one of the many that had and were to fall to the *Seeadler*'s guns.

It was true that several German captains, operating in ships like the *Seeadler* under the guise of innocent merchantmen, had been quite ruthless in their tactics. Some of them would not tolerate taking on the extra burden of prisoners and sent Allied crews to their fate in open boats in the tempestuous Atlantic ocean. But this accusation could never be levelled at Count von Lückner. Here was a man who fought his war, and won his victories, by trick and cunning, but in spite of his success he did not take the life of one single human being. He conducted his war in the *Seeadler* with the manners and fair play of a true gentleman, who would sacrifice himself rather than take another's life. Amid the terrible carnage of the First World War, a man like von Lückner shone out like a saint. The story of von Lückner's epic cruise in the *Seeadler* is the more remarkable for it was the very people whom he took prisoner who were to sing his praises after the war was over. Felix von Lückner's love of the sea began at a very early age and he longed, all through his childhood, for the day when he would be able to 'sign on' and begin the great adventure of a seaman, putting into ports at the farthest corners of the world. But alas, his parents had other plans for Felix. He was the son of a nobleman, and his father did not believe it fitting for a boy of his to join the navy. However, Felix was not to be swayed in his determination and at the age of thirteen, he packed a bag and ran off to the sea where he served before the mast in several sailing ships, one of which was British—a ship he was to meet up with some years later under very different circumstances. But in the meantime von Lückner hankered after a career in the Imperial German Navy, and longed to get aboard one of his country's giant warships, and so it was that he enlisted and worked his way up through the lower-deck until he reached the rank of lieutenant commander. By then he had taken his father's title, Count Felix von Lückner.

Von Lückner saw action at Jutland and after that epic encounter with the British Fleet, when the fate of the German Fleet was sealed, the High Command had to think of a new way of striking at the British merchant-marine, now that the fleet was 'bottled-up' in port. It was then that the idea of the commerce raider was given serious thought. Some ingenious strategist thought that if the navy could commandeer some merchantmen and secrete guns on board them and get through the British blockade into the Atlantic, they could play havoc with Britain's supply ships sailing across the Atlantic with vital war materials. An innocent merchantman, flying the flag of a neutral country, would not, they hoped, be suspected of

31

becoming a formidable weapon. On paper the idea looked good and it was put into action.

Von Lückner was one of those chosen to command a commerce raider and, because of his experience under sail, he was given the *Seeadler*. Nothing could have pleased him more and he set about making the necessary modifications to his new ship. His first thought was speed. To be really effective the *Seeadler* could not afford to rely on her sails, so he installed a 1,000 horse-power motor. Then he fitted her with two guns which were hidden inside the ship. When about to go into action these guns could be brought up behind the ship's rail which was hinged so that, when the guns were needed, the rail could be pushed away.

The most important part of any ship is its crew. Von Lückner chose each one of his men with infinite care. Some of them had served with him before, some he knew of by repute, and others he had never met. But they all had one thing in common . . . they were tough, well-disciplined and seasoned sailors.

When von Lückner had put the final touches to his new command he reported that he was ready to sail, and one morning in December 1916, the *Seeadler* weighed anchor and set sail out of Hamburg. Von Lückner paced the deck of his new command as a strong North Sea wind drove her forward through the waves towards the English Channel. His thoughts were on the encounter that he would inevitably have with the British navy when he passed through the Channel. The Royal Navy had sealed up the North Sea with its warships patrolling its exits, and von Lückner knew that his only chance of getting through the blockade and into the Atlantic would be to bluff his way out.

Nothing had been left to chance. He was sailing

under the Norwegian flag and had gone to great lengths to make his ship resemble a Norwegian cargo boat, even to the extent of dressing-up one of his sailors as the captain's wife to lend credence to his story.

At last the time came when he was challenged by a British cruiser and ordered to stop. While the British examined his ship, luckily not taking the trouble to board her, the tension on board was almost unbearable. Had he thought of everything? Perhaps he had overlooked some minor detail that would give him away? Thoughts like these raced through his mind, and at any second he expected the cruiser's guns to roar into life and blast his ship out of the water. But such was not to be his fate. The British captain gave him the all clear and von Lückner set off again under full sail, relieved that perhaps the greatest ordeal he would have to face was over.

The *Seeadler* ploughed her way out into the Atlantic and von Lückner's epic voyage got underway. He soon discovered just how effective his commerce raider was to be. Before he had left Germany he had been given orders that he was to confine his activities to sinking British sailing ships because it was considered that his windjammer would be ineffective against a steamer. Von Lückner proved his advisers wrong when the first ship he sent sent to the bottom was a British steamer.

From then on more and more ships fell victim to his ruse and in the first two months of his Atlantic mission he sank no less than eleven ships, which represented around 40,000 tons of shipping.

But this remarkable success did provide him with a problem. The more ships he sank, the more prisoners he took on board and some of his captives were ladies. It was typical of von Lückner to be concerned for them and he did all he could to make their ordeal more bearable, including throwing champagne parties and having his own crew entertain the prisoners with songs and dances! In fact, so relaxed was the atmosphere on board the *Seeadler* that von Lückner gave the prisoners almost the run of the ship. But even von Lückner knew that it could not last. Somehow he had to off-load his charges and put them ashore so that he could get on with the job of being a commerce raider. He knew, however, that the moment he landed them they would blurt out the story and the secret of the *Seeadler* would remain no longer. With her secret out and the Allied shipping warned of her presence, her effectiveness as a raider would disappear. He mulled over the problem in his mind until he came up with an idea.

Von Lückner intercepted the French bark *Cambronne* off the coast of South America and he transferred all his prisoners to her. But he had to make sure that they did not reach port too quickly, otherwise the game would be up and he would be hotly pursued by British or American warships, so he cut off the *Cambronne*'s top-gallant masts and bowsprit to slow her down, then sent her on her way to Rio de Janeiro. It was a relieved but sad band of ex-prisoners who waved von Lückner farewell from the deck of the *Cambronne*.

Now von Lückner had to find a new hunting ground and he struck on the idea of heading for the Pacific Ocean and trying his luck there. With the United States now in the war, her merchant ships were fair game for the commerce raider, so he headed for Cape Horn which is regarded by many sailors as the most hazardous stretch of sea in the world. In fair weather the Horn is a dangerous place to be, and it is a tribute to von Lückner's seamanship that when he took the *Seeadler* round it, he did so in the teeth of a hurricane. Not many men had ever done so in a sailing ship and lived to tell the tale.

Once in the Pacific he set about his piratical activities once more with the same gallantry he had shown in the Atlantic. The cruise of the *Seeadler* was soon to come to an end but not, as one might have expected, at the hands of the Allies. It was the sea that finally claimed the windjammer . . .

The *Seeadler* had been at war for almost twenty months when one day, in 1918, in the South Pacific she was lying off an atoll. She had many prisoners aboard from successful interceptions and von Lückner was well pleased with his success. But as he came on deck that morning he saw the ominous signs of a storm brewing. In what seemed like no time at all, the sea was whipped into a fury by a violent wind and an enormous tidal wave charged towards the ship. It grew larger and larger as it raced towards them until it towered high above the ship. It seemed to hang above them for a moment, gathering its strength to destroy, then it crashed down on the *Seeadler* breaking her up like matchwood. As the mammoth wave swept away von Lückner took stock of what was left of his ship. She was sinking but miraculously everyone had survived. Like the true sailor he was, he remained calm and got everyone into boats before leaving the ship himself and rowing to the shore.

When he reached the safety of the atoll he had the heart-rending experience of watching his beloved ship being smashed up as the heavy seas pounded her on to the reef. The *Seeadler* was no more but von Lückner was by no means finished with the war. He was determined that he, his crew and his prisoners were not going to rot away on that lonely atoll. In any case he had been sent to sea to do a job and his country was still at war.

The Count fitted out a life-boat and chose five of his sturdiest men as crew, then set off to find another island and a ship. The intrepid mariner eventually found an island where he convinced the authorities that he and his men were Norwegians and all he wanted was a passage home. He was allowed to stay on the island and he approached the captain of a British sailing ship who agreed to take him and his men on as crew. Nothing could have pleased von Lückner more and he drew up a plan to overpower the British crew and take command, so that he could resume his commerce raiding activities again. But alas, however daring the plan was, it was never to be put into effect. Their ship was only a few hundred yards from the shore when a fast motor launch sped out to them—packed with troops. The game was up. Von Lückner and his men were duly taken prisoner and transported to an island prison off the coast of New Zealand. But the von Lückner saga was far from over.

One night he and his men crept down to the pier and stole the prison warden's personal motor-boat, racing off into the night as fast as the boat could carry them. In fact their escape was so successful that they actually succeeded in capturing a sailing boat and put to sea, determined to take up where they had left off with the *Seeadler*. But their luck was not to hold.

The Royal New Zealand Navy was scouring the sea for them and the inevitable happened—von Lückner was caught. A cruiser charged in on his ship and the gallant Count realised that shooting it out was utterly out of the question. He surrendered and was shipped off to a more secure prison camp.

A few months after the war ended in 1918, von

Lückner was released and returned to Germany and a hero's welcome. When, sometime later, he visited England, he got an equally enthusiastic welcome, particularly from the many British prisoners he had treated so well when they had been captives on board his ship. They realised only too well that, had their ships fallen to some German commander other than von Lückner, they might have suffered a much different fate.

The commerce raiding cruise of the *Seeadler* had lasted almost twenty months, and in that time von Lückner had sunk more than £5,000,000-worth of Allied shipping—without the loss of one single life. Count Felix von Lückner must rank amongst the most gallant and gentlemanly 'pirates' ever to sail the sea.

* * * *

The Imperial German Navy was not the only one to use the seemingly-innocent merchant ship as a lure for its prey. The Royal Navy operated a fleet of such ships, which it designated 'Q' ships, and a wide variety of vessels were used for the job. But the task of the British Q-ships differed considerably from that of their German counterparts in that their job was to combat the ever-increasing menace of the German U-boat. During the First World War, U-boats played havoc with Allied shipping in the Atlantic sending hundreds of thousands of tons of ships to the bottom. The Q-ships were intended to lure the U-boats to the surface by their innocent appearance and blast them out of the water. Some thought that these Q-ships would be no match for the submarine, but, as will be seen, they met with considerable success.

One Spring evening in 1917, Count Spiegel, the

captain of the German submarine U-93, scanned the Atlantic horizon through his periscope as the U-boat nosed along just beneath the surface. Suddenly he stopped and focussed on a schooner under full sail. A modest prize, he thought, but nevertheless one which he could not let slip through his fingers. The schooner, small as it was and apparently unarmed, did not merit a torpedo, so he surfaced and fired three shots across her bows. Immediately the schooner came to a halt and Spiegel could see clearly the crew taking to the boats. He laughed and turned to a grim-faced man standing beside him in the conning tower.

'This one will be easy,' Spiegel said.

The man beside him wore the uniform of a captain of the British Merchant Marine. He was Captain Burroughs whose ship Spiegel had sunk some days earlier off the Canadian coast. Burroughs did not share Spiegel's enthusiasm for the 'easy' kill. He watched the schooner's crew desperately pull away from the ship to allow the German captain to get on with his dirty work. He was tempted to avert his eyes but he could not help but watch this majestic sailing ship in the last few minutes of her life.

'Fire!' Spiegel's yell echoed from the conning tower and the U-boat's gun roared, hurling a shell through the air. It smashed into the target followed by more shells until the schooner was on fire. Spiegel, in his eagerness, ordered his boat closer to the schooner and she edged forward. But as she did so, Spiegel uttered a cry . . .

'*Mein Gott!*' he bellowed as a white ensign unfurled at the top of the main mast. A split second later, the bulwarks fell away and Spiegel found himself staring into the muzzles of two 12-pounder guns and two Lewis guns.

'It's a trap!' Spiegel shouted, horror-stuck. He did not get the opportunity to order the sub to crash-dive for all four guns on board the schooner opened up plastering the U-boat's conning tower with shells and raking it with machine-gun fire. In an instant men were mown down while others were blasted clear off the U-boat's casing. Burroughs dived headlong down into the conning tower while Spiegel was thrown into the air and hit the water as another shell exploded near the tower.

Spiegel thrashed about in the water, cursing himself for falling into the trap as more shells whistled over his head and crashed into the U-boat. He was to be even angrier when the lifeboat launched from the schooner picked him up and he discovered the schooner was none other than HMS *Prize*—a German ship which had been captured by the British shortly after the outbreak of the war. The man behind the guns on *Prize* was Lieutenant Sanders and he and his gun crews kept up the barrage of fire until U-93 managed to limp away into the darkness.

As the U-boat disappeared, Sanders and his men dashed from the guns to stem the tide of flames that was engulfing the ship and plug the holes through which the sea was rushing into the ship's hold. After a frantic battle against sea and flame they finally succeeded in preventing the schooner from sinking and Spiegel and the other survivors from U-93 were hauled aboard. In spite of his fury at being tricked, Spiegel could not help but admire the courage of the young Lieutenant for holding his fire so long, waiting until the time for his attack was right while he took the full force of the German gun fire.

Both the *Prize* and U-93 managed to limp back to their home bases. From the *Prize* Count Spiegel went to spend the remainder of the war in a prisoner-of-war camp in England, while Captain Burroughs did likewise in Germany. But before Count Spiegel was incarcerated he went to great lengths to sing the praises of Lieutenant Sanders for his courage, and even went to the extent of suggesting that he should be awarded the country's highest award for gallantry. He was and Lieutenant Sanders was decorated with the Victoria Cross.

After a refit, *Prize* put to sea once more, this time with Sanders promoted to Lieutenant Commander in command. But she was sunk by a German U-boat and lost with all hands.

*   *   *   *

The greatest exponent of the use of the Q-ship was Rear-Admiral Gordon Campbell, VC. By June 1917 he had already won the Victoria Cross in a gallant Q-ship action and he was yet again to show his special qualities of courage in an epic action which earned two men their country's highest accolade.

On 7 June 1917, Campbell was in command of the Q-ship, *Pargust*, sailing off the coast of Ireland when a U-boat slid towards him at periscope depth. The U-boat commander was in a quandary. The ship he saw through his periscope certainly looked like a tramp steamer and it mounted a gun which two seamen were busily polishing. (This 'gun' was in fact a dummy which Campbell had mounted on deck in the hope that it might make the enemy less suspicious of the guns that lay hidden.) But the U-boat commander was still not satisfied that the tramp was genuine. He had heard too many stories of his comrades falling victim to British trickery and he decided to take no chances and fired a torpedo at the *Pargust*. It struck the Q-ship and exploded, tearing a 40-foot hole in the ship's side just above the water-line and killing one of the crew. As the ship rocked in the waves tons of water flooded in through the gash and it seemed that she was doomed. But Campbell was determined that the U-boat would not get off with its attack. He swung into action ordering the 'dummy crew' to abandon ship and the U-boat commander soon saw men rushing for the lifeboats while the gun crew on the fake deck-gun acted out the loading procedure. But they too soon 'panicked' and ran for the boats.

Within a few minutes the boats were pulling away from the *Pargust*. But while they were doing so Campbell and his real gun crews were lying flat on the decks ready to man the guns when the time came. Through a slit in the bulwarks Campbell could see the 'eye' of the periscope peering just above the surface. He knew that if the German had the slightest suspicion that the tramp was anything but deserted, then he would finish the job with another torpedo. Then, at last, after an agonising wait, the U-boat surfaced but no-one appeared at her conning tower. Still the German was not sure.

Campbell had to have the U-boat's crew on deck before he would chance firing. By doing that, he would make sure that the sub would find it difficult to crash-dive quickly with the hatches open. Then he realised that the lifeboats were drifting between the *Pargust* and the U-boat. When he did open fire his own men would be smack in the line of fire. Luckily the men in the lifeboats had the same thought and they rowed out of the way. A few moments later the U-boat commander appeared at the conning tower. Now was Campbell's chance to strike.

The bulwarks fell away and the guns blazed into life. The first salvo smashed the conning tower, leaving it a twisted, mangled, tangle of jagged metal. More shells thudded into the submarine, puncturing the casing as some of the crew scrambled on to the deck, raising their arms in the air in surrender. When Campbell caught sight of them he yelled:

'Cease fire!'

But no sooner had the guns fallen silent than the submarine made a dash to escape and as she did so, the men on the outer-casing were washed into the sea. In an instant *Pargust*'s guns opened up once more, lashing the submarine with fire. Then a shell ripped through the U-boat and hit the load of mines she was carrying. The resulting explosion tore the submarine wide open and she sank. The battle was over and *Pargust* had won the day. Only two men survived from the U-boat.

Pargust was so badly damaged that she had to radio for help and was towed to port where she underwent repairs. When the Admiralty heard of the courage of Campbell and his men they made an award of £1,000 to the entire crew. But there was more to follow. It was decided that two VCs would be awarded to the ship's company and a ballot was held to decide who should receive them on behalf of the crew. They chose Lieutenant R. N. Stuart and Seaman William Williams. It was Williams who, after the torpedo had struck the *Pargust* and dislodged a huge plate hiding one of the guns, held that plate in position until Campbell gave the order to fire. Had Williams not held that plate in place, *Pargust*'s secret would have been revealed and the result of the battle quite different.

3

The Charioteers

Darkness hung like a black shroud over the port of Pola, on the Adriatic Sea, embracing ships of the Austrian fleet lying at anchor in the harbour one night in 1918.

On a pier near the harbour entrance a sentry paced his 'beat', pausing occasionally to allow his eyes to scan the huge, fat hulks that lay almost motionless in the water. Among them was the 20,000-ton super-dreadnought *Viribus Unitas*, a giant of a ship bristling with guns and a long sought-after target for the Italian navy.

As the sentry continued his vigil he pondered on the bloody conflict that had raged in Europe for four long years. There seemed to be no end to the senseless slaughter. Millions of men had already perished in the trenches, in the air, and at sea and even more had been wounded, some never to recover, some to die many years later from these wounds.

The sentry cursed his lot and mouthed an oath of contempt for the political leaders who had drawn his country into war. Had he but known it then, peace was just a few days away. But before that night was out an historic action was to take place under his very nose—an attack that was to bring a new concept to naval strategy.

Far out at sea an Italian launch sped through the waves, towing behind it what must have been one of the strangest battle-craft ever to take to water. It was half submarine, half surface craft, the brain-child of two Italian naval officers, Surgeon-Lieutenant Paolucci and Major Raffaele Rossetti.

The concept behind this underwater vehicle was simple in theory. It was designed to travel just below the surface of the water with its two-man crew riding it like a horse with their heads sticking just above water. The aft part of the one-and-a-half-ton craft housed the power unit, a compressed-air engine capable of pushing it through the water for a short period at about two knots—a perilously slow and vulnerable speed for a ship of war. The forepart of the craft was detachable and contained two mines, each packed with 350 lbs of TNT explosives. The object was to penetrate enemy harbour defences, detach the mines and attach them, like limpets, to the hulls of enemy ships. A tiny clockwork detonating device on the mine was pre-set to allow the swimmer time to get well out of the way before it exploded.

That, at least, was the plan but as our intrepid warriors were to discover to their cost, the best-laid schemes do not always work out as planned.

On board the launch, Rossetti and Paolucci stripped off their clothes until they were left wearing only swimsuits. The bite of the cold night air sent a shiver through their bodies as the launch and its motors came to a halt.

The two men were about to embark on one of the most courageous and hazardous missions of the war—a two man attack on the Austrian fleet. Their object was to penetrate the series of harbour defences and plant their mines on two of the ships that lay at anchor there.

As the chariot was pulled alongside the launch and the two men dropped into the icy-cold water to board

44

it, the crew of the launch wished them luck, knowing only too well that there was little chance of the two charioteers returning from their mission alive.

The captain of the launch waved as he turned his boat and headed out ot sea once more, leaving the two men alone with their chariot. With the compressed-air engine going full-out Rossetti and Paolucci ploughed laboriously through the rolling sea towards the black shape of the hostile coastline—unaware of the extent of the danger that lay ahead. The agonising wait to get into action tested their nerves to the limit until soaked through, with their bones chilled to the marrow, they were within a few yards of the harbour entrance.

It was here that they sighted their first obstacle, a row of empty 10-foot long metal drums floating like a chain strung across the harbour entrance, forming a barrier between them and their target. Talking in whispers, Paolucci and Rossetti puzzled over how they were to overcome this seemingly impossible obstacle. The chariot could not dive beneath the drums because they would almost certainly drown or lose the chariot altogether. It seemed that there was only one solution. They would have to get their craft *over* the top of the chain of drums . . . and that is precisely what they did.

Both men slid into the water and, with every muscle in their bodies straining, they pushed and pulled the chariot, inch by inch, over the drums—all one and a half tons of it! Exhausted, but elated at beating the barrier, they clambered aboard their chariot once more and headed farther into the harbour.

As they slid onward beneath the waves, the two men could hear the far-off, familiar sound of a working harbour and their hearts beat faster as they finally distinguished the dark shapes of the Austrian ships. But time was running out. Their engine had only a limited life and they decided they would have to give their craft a helping hand. Both men slid off and got behind the chariot—and pushed.

They struggled with all their might to shove the cumbersome craft forward but without much effect. Then suddenly they both froze, as they heard the noise of approaching engines. They peered desperately into the darkness, trying to catch sight of the craft. All sorts of crazy thoughts raced through their minds— worst of all the prospect of being rammed. Just then they caught sight of it—a submarine on the surface sliding down the harbour channel out towards the sea.

It seemed as if they must be spotted. There was only one thing to do, they thought. At the least sign of discovery, they would detonate the mines and blast the chariot—and themselves—to bits. Above all, they could not allow the chariot to fall into enemy hands or future operations would be doomed to failure.

Hardly daring to breathe they trod water and watched, with only their heads above the water, as the submarine rode past them. Miraculously, they remained unnoticed. They couldn't believe their luck as the sub disappeared out of sight and into the darkness. Their spirits rose once more and they got underway, heading deeper into the harbour.

As they struggled on, the risk of detection became greater. The Austrians had gone to great lengths to protect their precious fleet—as the next obstacle was to prove.

Ahead of the two charioteers lay an enormous thick, wooden gate, capable of being opened to allow ships to pass through out to the open sea. As they neared it, a ship approached and the gate slowly creaked open. This was their chance but there was a problem. At one side of the gate a guard-ship was anchored while at the other side on the pier stood the sentry, his thoughts still on the everlasting war. They couldn't turn back now—a more opportune moment might never arise again so they had no choice but to take a chance and press on.

As luck would have it, the heavens opened and rain poured down from the black sky. On the pier, the sentry raised his collar and slid into the doorway of a nearby building while Paolucci and Rossetti rode through the gap. But their troubles were far from over. They had no sooner got through the gate when they were faced with yet another obstacle—a series of three rows of steel cables. Once more they had to push the chariot over them. By then the current was becoming dangerously fast and they had to summon up yet more strength to battle against it. Finally they encountered the last barrier—another triple net and once more they succeeded in shoving and pushing the cumbersome craft across it by sheer brute force.

At last they were in the harbour proper but by then they had used up so much time that their plan had already failed in part. It was 3 am—the exact time when they were supposed to have rendezvoused with the launch out at sea. There was no escape by the sea route now. But they did not despair. Having come this far they were determined to pull off the job.

Utterly exhausted, the two men sat astride the chariot and surveyed the scene before them. There lay the cream of the Austrian naval fleet—a horde of naval units, six of them capital ships and the largest of them all, the 20,000-ton super dreadnought. It did not take the two men long to decide upon the ship they should attack—they would go for the *Viribus Unitas*. She lay at anchor in the far side of the harbour;

no matter, the Italians were determined that the warship was going to fall victim to their mines.

But however elated they were at the prospect of such a prize they were still to face problems. The rain poured mercilessly down and, worse still, the compressed-air engine on their chariot began to cough and splutter and to their horror the whole craft began to sink. The immersion valve had jammed open and it took all their combined strength to close it and keep the chariot on the surface.

By then they were nearing the dreadnought and Rossetti set about detaching one of the mines. Sapped of almost all his strength he could hardly budge it but at last he succeeded in prising it free and he swam off towards the towering hull of the *Viribus Unitas*. In the shadow of the ship he got to work clamping the mine on to the hull and set the clockwork delayed-action mechanism before swimming away as fast as he could. Part of his job was done but it had taken him more than thirty minutes and it was an anxious Paolucci who spotted him fighting his way back towards the chariot through the water. He pulled his comrade aboard but he had no sooner done so than the whole area was a blaze of light. They had been spotted and the powerful searchlight from the bridge of the *Viribus Unitas* captured them in its beam. The game was up but however hopeless their chances of escape were, they were by no means finished. Hurriedly they slid into the water and set the chariot careering off on its own towards a merchant ship lying not far off. Moments later there was a thundering roar as the second mine on the craft found its mark and within minutes the merchant ship sank. Already the two Italians had caused chaos . . . but there was more to come.

As they were hauled aboard the *Viribus Unitas*

48

Rossetti's mine attached to the hull was ticking away. There was barely half an hour to go before the mine was due to explode.

Meanwhile they scrambled over the ship's rail and to their horror saw that the caps the sailors wore bore the word 'Yugoslavia.' They couldn't believe their eyes but they were soon put in the picture. Only a few hours before they had launched their attack there had been a revolt aboard the ship. Now Yugoslavians and not enemy Austrians were in command. Both the Italians knew immediately what they must do. They were brought before the new commander of the ship, Captain Voukovich, and they told him what they had done.

The captain lost no time in ordering his crew to abandon ship and they poured over the side like lemmings, plunging into the water. In the confusion, Rossetti and Paolucci made good their escape but they were not to remain at liberty for long. Once in the water some of the Yugoslavs decided that the whole thing was a hoax and in spite of the Italians' protests to the contrary they were taken back aboard the ship.

The Yugoslavs were soon to discover just how wrong they had been when, with a thundering roar, the mine exploded. The ship lurched violently and began to sink and without hesitation the crew took to the boats, all, that is, except the captain who, true to naval tradition, stayed with his ship. As a parting gesture of respect for the gallant Italians who had so daringly attacked his ship, he shook both of them by the hand. Minutes later, the two Italians had the heart-rending experience of watching the *Viribus Unitas* topple and sink.

Paolucci and Rossetti were put aboard a hospital ship to recover from their ordeal and it was from their cabin that, five days later, they watched the Italian fleet sail into Pola harbour. Italy was at peace with Austria. The Armistice had been signed.

Later the two intrepid charioteers returned to Italy to the heroes' welcome they so richly deserved but for them their home-coming was tinged with sadness. They had witnessed a gallant captain go to his death and when Rossetti was later awarded £15,000 by the Italian government he donated all of it to Captain Voukovich's widow and a fund for the wives of other of his former enemies who had lost their lives.

*   *   *   *

Although at long last the world was, mercifully, at peace once more, the daring exploits and experiments in this revolutionary kind of naval warfare by Paolucci and Rossetti were not to be forgotten—a fact that was to cost the British Royal and Merchant Navies dearly, years later.

Two Italian naval architects, Sub-lieutenants Tesei and Toschi, inspired by the success of Rossetti and Paolucci, worked day and night on plans for a more sophisticated type of underwater craft and, in 1935, they submitted drawings to the Italian Naval High Command. Admiral Cavagnari, remembering the success of the World War One raid, ordered work to begin immediately on building a prototype.

The new 'chariot' resembled a cigar-shaped torpedo, 22 feet in length and 21 inches in diameter with a detachable warhead packed with 500 pounds of explosives. At the rear of this 'long-range torpedo', as it was designated, were two propellers driven by batteries. The two-man crew sat astride the torpedo with the pilot in front at the controls with which he could steer and regulate the depth of the craft using the compressed air tanks.

Along with this new craft came another invention which was to make it even more effective than its predecessor—the first underwater breathing apparatus. This allowed the crew to submerge and approach their target unseen. Exhaustive tests were carried out in Italian harbours until volunteer crews had been trained and problems with the craft itself ironed out. But while these tests were in progress, Europe was once more plunged into world war for the second time in half a century and Italy's new underwater weapon was to be used with devastating effect.

There followed two unsuccessful attacks on the British naval base at Gibraltar, one in 1940 and one the following year when Tesei, one of the inventors, was captured. The cat was out of the bag and at last the British were wise to the Italians' plans. If another attack was to come the British would be ready. Special British naval units were formed comprised of expert swimmers and divers whose job it was to search the underwater hulls of ships coming into harbour and disarm limpet mines, or war-heads attached to them.

The men chosen for this task required the highest form of courage, nerves of steel and a complete disregard for their own safety. To add more menace to their work, the Italians had recruited men who posed as seamen in neutral ports. Their clandestine job was to 'plant' delayed-action limpet mines on the hulls of Allied ships, set to explode while the ships were at sea.

The Italians, however, had yet to pull off a successful chariot attack. They had not long to wait . . .

On the night of 18/19 September, 1941, the Italian submarine *Scire* slipped, unseen, into the Bay of

Gibraltar. Anchored to the hull of the sub were three chariots.

Captain Borghese, commander of the *Scire*, peered anxiously into his periscope and swung it round 360 degrees. The coast was clear and the submarine rose to the surface amid a turmoil of bubbling water. As the water washed off the deck, the eager seamen scrambled out of the conning tower and lowered the three chariots into the sea. Then the crews of the chariots emerged from the tower on deck clad in their rubber frogman suits looking like creatures from another planet. One by one they scrambled on to their respective chariots and began the four-mile voyage to their target.

In the lead chariot, Lieutenant Visintini set course for the harbour with the chariot submerged just below the surface which allowed him and his crewman, Magro, to conserve their vital oxygen supply by breathing fresh air. Ahead of him Visintini could see the familiar shape of the towering Rock of Gibraltar.

'This time,' he thought, 'we shall succeed!' and the chariots nosed their way through the water, deeper into the bay.

It was almost 6 am on 19 September when Visintini's chariot reached the first obstacle lying in its path into the harbour—the anti-submarine nets. He had come prepared for this by bringing along a set of compressed-air cutters but, as luck would have it, he had no need for them. He caught sight of a British destroyer approaching the harbour and cunningly slipped into the harbour behind it when the nets were drawn open.

He had succeeded in penetrating the defences of what was claimed to be the safest harbour in the world.

Cautiously the chariot inched its way deeper into

the harbour until Visintini saw what he had been looking for—the naval tanker *Denbydale*. He signalled to Magro that he was going to dive. Their heads disappeared under water and, steering on a compass-bearing, the chariot slid towards the tanker.

Visintini strained his eyes to catch sight of the bottom of the *Denbydale*. Then, through the murky water it was there, above them. He manoeuvred the chariot beneath the ship and stopped engines. They had reached their goal.

Visintini blew water out of the diving tanks and the craft rose until it touched the ship's bottom. Then he set about the task of finding the bilge keel, the wide ledge that runs around the hull of every ship. When he had finally edged the craft into position, Magro fixed a long line to the keel by means of a clamp. With that done, Visintini edged the chariot underneath the *Denbydale* once more and up to the other side where Magro fixed the other end of the line to the bilge keel, again using a clamp. Nosing the chariot back to the middle of the line, Visintini detached the explosive-packed war-head, set the delayed-action detonating device, then attached the war-head to the line so that it dangled beneath the ship. The job was done but they had to get out of the harbour unseen—or this journey would have been wasted.

Visintini's skill as a submariner was shown when he succeeded in slipping out of the harbour by diving under the anti-submarine net and out into the open sea.

Not long after their escape the *Denbydale* rocked as 500 pounds of explosives shattered her underplates. Minutes later, out in the Bay of Gibraltar, the 2,444-ton tanker *Fiona Shell* and the 10,900-ton cargo vessel *Durham* both lurched crazily, seriously damaged by explosives. The other Italian crews had also succeeded in their missions.

All three crews managed to reach neutral Spain from where they were flown to Italy and a tumultuous welcome. There was no longer any doubt that the Italians had a devastatingly effective weapon and the Allies (in particular the British) were seriously worried. Then, three months later, as if to rub salt into the wound, the Italians attempted the most audacious attack of all—against the British battleships *Queen Elizabeth* and *Valiant*.

Once more, the submarine *Scire* was the vehicle which brought three human torpedoes to the scene of the action.

Valiant was the target for the chariot commanded by Count Luigi de la Pene and his number two, Bianchi. While the other two torpedoes headed for their targets, one to *Queen Elizabeth* and the other to a naval tanker, de la Pene steered towards the *Valiant* then dived. But as he dived Bianchi was swept off the chariot and had to swim for his life to a nearby buoy which he clung on to desperately. De la Pene went on alone and reached the *Valiant* where he deposited the war-head on the sea bed beneath the hull. He then scuttled the chariot and swam to the surface where he saw Bianchi clinging to the buoy. Within seconds of him breaking the surface, they were spotted and taken aboard *Valiant* where they were brought face to face with Captain Morgan the ship's commander.

Try as he might, Captain Morgan could not get the Italians to reveal their reason for being in the water near his ship, but he had a pretty good idea. He reasoned that if he put the two men down in the bottom-most part of the ship and they had attached explosives to the hull, they would be quick to tell him. It was a chance he had

54

to take, playing on their nerves. De la Pene and Bianchi were led below and locked in a compartment deep down in the ship. The seconds ticked by. For two long, nerve-racking hours they sat there waiting for the blast that would spell their end, while Captain Morgan waited for them to crack, but he had reckoned without their courage. Morgan waited and waited, until he received a message from de la Pene telling him that his ship would blow up in five minutes' time.

Morgan immediately ordered his crew on to the deck and, just as the five minutes were up, the charge exploded severely damaging the ship's bottom. None of those on board, including de la Pene and Bianchi was injured. Had Morgan only known that the mine was *not* in fact attached to the ship he could have saved it, simply by moving the ship.

The explosion that rocked the *Valiant* was closely followed by two more. All three chariots had found their targets.

The Italians' courage greatly impressed Captain Morgan and later in 1945 after the Italian surrender, he attended the ceremony at which the Italian government awarded de la Pene his country's highest award for gallantry, the *Medaglio d'Oro*. Morgan counted it a privilege when he was permitted to pin the medal on de la Pene's chest himself.

*   *   *   *

The Italian human torpedo attacks continued with ever-increasing effect and more and more British ships fell victim to these clandestine raids—largely because of a brilliant scheme thought up by Lieutenant Visintini. He knew of an Italian tanker, the 4,000 ton *Olterra*, which had been scuttled by its crew in the

Spanish port of Algeciras at the outbreak of the war. Instead of having to rely upon a vulnerable submarine to carry the human torpedoes within striking distance of their target, why not a secret, permanent base from which the torpedo crews could launch their attacks? The *Olterra*, Visintini reckoned, was just what he had been looking for. It was conveniently situated in a neutral country. He devised a cover-story to give the Spanish authorities should they come snooping around at the first sign of activity on board the *Olterra*. They were to be told the ship was undergoing repairs so that she would be fit for sea when the war was over.

So it was that, late in 1942, Italian 'engineers' began work on the *Olterra*. But, far from repairing her, they made pretty sure that she would not be fit to go to sea again by cutting a 25-foot long section in the bulkhead separating the bow compartment from the cargo hold, then they hinged it so that it hung like a flap. With that done they pumped water out of the forward tanks until the bows rose clear of the water. A four-foot hole, also hinged, was cut in the side of the ship opening into the bow compartment and about 6 feet below the normal waterline.

When the ship returned to its normal position, the hold was dry and the bow compartment flooded. The two-man torpedoes were assembled in the hold so that they could be lowered into the bow and then pass out of the ship through the hinged flap six feet below water.

The Italians then smuggled two-man torpedo parts into Spain and the *Olterra* base became operational. The effect was devastating and the Italians took a terrible toll of ships anchored at Gibraltar. Alas, during one of the attacks Visintini, the architect of the *Olterra* plan, was killed. He was later buried at sea by the British with full military honours.

The *Olterra* base remained a secret until after Italy's surrender in 1943 when British Naval officers visited it. Staggered at what they found they were the first to praise the cunning and daring of these gallant Italian seamen who had gone to war on iron chariots.

4

U-Boat Attack

On 3 September 1939, Europe was plunged into war for the second time in less than fifty years when Britain declared war on Germany following the Nazi invasion of Poland. On that very same day, only a few hours after war had been declared, a German submarine commander perpetrated one of the worst crimes in the annals of naval history.

The Second World War was barely a day old when Lieutenant Commander Lemp, captain of the German submarine U-30, peered through his periscope and focussed on the dark shape of a ship rolling in the waves off the Irish coast. Lemp's eyes lit up as he ordered his crew to action stations. His would be the first U-boat to strike a blow for the Fatherland; little did he realise that the repercussions of the 'blow' he was about to deal Britain were to reverberate throughout the world.

At that time there were very strict rules laid down under international law regarding the sinking of enemy shipping during wartime and there was no excuse for a seasoned submarine commander like

Lemp not to know them to the letter. His instructions were clear when dealing with enemy ships, particularly merchantmen. He must first surface and halt the ship then examine it. If it was seen to be carrying a cargo which could be classified as contraband, then the submarine commander was entitled to sink it, but not before ensuring the safety of the merchantman's crew by taking them aboard his own ship.

The only occasions when a submarine commander could order an attack on an enemy ship without prior warning was when it either refused to halt when called to do so, was sailing under escort by aircraft or armed ships, resisted when called to halt, or was a troopship. Lemp knew these rules and knew them well, as every other U-boat commander did. He was also aware, however, that if he did surface to inspect the merchantman, he would lay himself open to attack if the enemy ship had concealed guns.

Lemp watched the British ship carefully, noting that she was steering a zig-zag course and knowing that she was out of the normal sea routes for ocean-going British ships. He formed the opinion that she must be a British troopship and was, therefore, fair game for his torpedoes. His mind was made up. He would attack. And with no further hesitation he fired a torpedo which struck the target and exploded, gashing the ship's hull. Within seconds, tons of water poured into the stricken vessel as terrified and shocked people onboard fought their way to the lifeboats while the wireless operator sent out an urgent SOS message.

It was only then that the horrible truth dawned on the U-boat commander. He had struck the British passenger liner *Athenia* which carried more than a thousand men, women and children. The frantic call for help was heard by ships in the vicinity and they changed course to come to the aid of the sinking liner, but while they charged through the waves on their mercy mission, Lemp's submarine scurried away from the scene, maintaining radio silence as he had been ordered by the German High Command.

Just before noon the following day, the *Athenia* sank taking with her 112 people, including women and children, twenty-eight of whom were American nationals. The German U-boat service had struck its first murderous blow.

The uproar that followed that attack on a ship unable to defend itself rocked the world and the propaganda machines of both Britain and Germany spouted forth their own versions of the incident. The British people could not believe that any sea captain could be so callous as to sink a defenceless ship. Nothing could have been more calculated to incense the British with hatred for their enemy than that single spineless act.

The British government was quick to accuse the Germans of waging unrestricted war against merchant shipping in complete contravention of all the existing international laws which determined the behaviour of submarines in wartime. Adolf Hitler, the German leader, like the British people, heard the news with total disbelief. For a time he refused to acknowledge that one of his commanders had disobeyed his strictest orders about attacking enemy shipping. It was Hitler's intention to do all he could to avoid an all-out confrontation with Britain, but the sinking of the *Athenia* so enraged the British people that all thoughts of ever reaching a peaceful settlement with Britain were forgotten.

To counter the British charge of atrocity, Doctor Josef Goebbels, Germany's Propaganda Minister, claimed that the sinking of the *Athenia* was an act of sabotage on the part of Winston Churchill, the First Lord of the Admiralty, who had arranged that the *Athenia* should be sunk at sea with the sacrifice of its crew and passengers in order to discredit the German Navy. The absurdity of Goebbels' claim would have been nothing short of laughable had it not concerned such a tragic matter, and it embittered the British even more towards the German people and their Nazi leaders.

It was not until late in September, when U-30 returned to her base, that the commander of the German submarine force, Kommodore Doenitz, learned the truth about what had happened. Even though Lemp had acted in good faith, imagining he was sinking an enemy troopship, Doenitz would not allow such an episode to remain in the submarine's diary and he ordered that the relevant page be replaced. But Doenitz could not blot out the shameful *Athenia* episode by erasing it from a ship's diary.

In the war years that followed, many thousands of tons of British and Allied shipping were sent to the bottom by German U-boats. But it must never be forgotten that this was precisely the task these submarines were given, the job of severing the vital life-line between the United Kingdom and North America. No one would justifiably deny that the vast majority of U-boat commanders and their crews fought a dangerous war with a courage and daring that would have done credit to any Allied submariner. It would be folly to suggest that, in general, the submarine tactics and strategy used by the German submarine force were in any way less noble than those employed by the British Navy and her allies.

After the *Athenia* affair, Hitler ordered that no

passenger ships were to be attacked. Only warships, merchant ships with air or ship escort or ships 'resisting arrest' were to be sunk without warning. U-boat captains were then careful to follow their Führer's orders to the letter.

On 5 September, only two days after the *Athenia* attack, the U-48, under the command of Lieutenant Commander Herbert Schultze, surfaced close to the British merchant ship *Royal Sceptre*. Adhering strictly to the rules, Schultze ordered her to halt by firing a shot across her bows. But the captain of *Royal Sceptre* wasn't having any of it. He ordered his wireless operator to call for assistance from British ships in the area, and turned his ship away, trying to make a run for it. Schultze then brought his 3·5-inch gun into action and scored hits on the British ship, forcing the crew to abandon ship and take to the boats. When he was sure that the crew of the British merchantman were safely in the boats, he sank the *Royal Sceptre* with a torpedo. But Schultze was far from finished. Later he sighted the British ship *Browning* and put a shot across her bows drawing her to a halt. The crew immediately took to their boats, only to be ordered back onboard by Schultze who instructed them to go to the aid of their comrades in the *Royal Sceptre*'s lifeboats! Hitler's submarine commanders were not going to risk the wrath of their Führer for disobeying orders.

They went about their task of sinking enemy ships with deadly efficiency, sending thousands of tons of merchant shipping to the bottom with guns and torpedoes. But the prize that the U-boat captains sought more than anything else at that time—the one that would bring them fame and acclaim—was to sink a British warship. It was not long in coming.

Lieutenant Commander Schuhardt, in U-29, hid

beneath the waves at periscope depth off the Bristol Channel in the Western Approaches to Britain, smack in the middle of the shipping lanes, waiting for enemy ships that might come his way. He scanned the horizon with his periscope and there framed in the ground disc of light was a 10,000-ton merchantman—an easy target. Overhead flew an aircraft escort so, according to the rules, he was justified in attacking. But as he lined up to launch his torpedoes, the ship turned away and steamed off at full speed, giving him a fast-moving and difficult target. He decided that he would wait until the liner was far off before surfacing and man-oeuvring at speed into a more advantageous position for an underwater attack. But as he took one final glance through the 'scope, Schuhardt spotted the blurred outline of a vessel on the horizon, steaming towards his position. The ship drew slowly closer and Schuhardt soon recognised the unmistakable shape of an aircraft carrier. It was the colossal HMS *Courageous*, a gigantic floating airfield slicing through the rolling seas. Fortune lay with Schuhardt for just as he was about to fire his torpedoes, the carrier turned, giving him her entire length to aim at.

Schuhardt fired three torpedoes at *Courageous* and they streaked through the sea towards the towering ship then struck with thunderous explosions, ripping the side of the carrier open. Instantly thousands of tons of water poured into the engine room and men fought to stem the flood, but *Courageous* was doomed and she listed drunkenly towards the sea. With her work done U-29 crash-dived when escorting destroyers raced in to seek out the attacker. Then, as the U-boat dived deeper, more explosions rocked the huge carrier when her boilers blew up.

The destroyer commanders were determined not to

let the submarine escape and they weaved about the area shooting off patterns of depth charges which plunged into the sea and exploded. Meanwhile the destroyers' Asdic beams probed the sea to locate the enemy submarine.

Asdic was a vital weapon fitted to destroyers to track down submarines. It was in many ways similar to the sensors used by bats for navigating through the sky. An electronic signal was transmitted down into the sea from the destroyer and if it hit a metal object, it bounced back. The Asdic operator could calculate the distance of the submarine according to the length of time the signal took to return to the ship. The longer the signal took the farther the submarine was from the searching destroyer. The cone of signal could be swung in a 360° arc and the Asdic operator could search the ocean and its bed for hours on end. The use of Asdic did, however, have its drawbacks. Shoals of fish tended to send back a signal and on many occasions ships were sent on crazy courses depth charging fish! But had it not been for Asdic, the British destroyers would have had nothing with which to seek out their enemy beneath the waves.

U-29 went deep and stayed there while the destroyers transformed the sea into a bubbling fury as they plastered the area with depth charges. Schuhard, waited until the coast was clear and made off, away from the scene where *Courageous* slid beneath the waves leaving the survivors amid the scattered flotsam. Of a crew of over one thousand, 519 men, including the captain, lost their lives. Schuhardt became a national hero overnight and on his return to base was greeted by the Führer himself. The Royal Navy had been dealt a serious blow but an even more catastrophic one was about to be felt when the German navy undertook a mission which must rank amongst the most daring in naval history.

Off the northernmost tip of the Scottish mainland lie the barren, wind-swept Orkney Islands, separated from Scotland by what is said by many sailors to be the most treacherous stretch of water anywhere in Britain, the Pentland Firth, with it racing tides and wild, tempestuous seas.

Almost desolate, rugged clumps of rocks, whittled out of the earth's crust, sit anchored in these raging seas. For thousands of years, wind, rain and tempest have tried their best to thrash the tiny islands out of existence but still they stand to weather the storm.

Five of the islands in that remote group, along with Orkney's own mainland, encircle a stretch of water known as Scapa Flow, which for almost half a century served as a base for the British Home Fleet and indeed became the graveyard of the German Fleet at the end of World War One. During that awful war the Flow formed a natural basin in which the British Fleet found succour when not in battle. When the German Fleet surrendered at the end of the war, it was ordered into Scapa and that was to be its last resting place. But if the British admiralty thought for one moment that it had captured a fleet of ships which it could convert into fighting ships for the Royal Navy, then it was quite wrong. When the entire fleet was safely tucked up in the Flow the German captains scuttled their ships leaving them as useless hulks on the sea-bed where some of them remain to this day. The German High Command had deprived Britain of a valuable prize and almost completely blocked the entrances to the Flow with their sunken ships. But unwittingly the German navy had provided the British Fleet with an even safer refuge which she could use when the Second

Above The British submarine E-11 and her crew get a heroes' welcome on their return from a triumphant foray in Turkish waters.

Left The damaged periscope of HM submarine E-11.

Above A British Q-ship. Outwardly she appeared an innocent merchantman but in reality she hid a deadly sting.

Right Captain Gordon Campbell, VC, seen here with his pet dog, was the most successful of all the British Q-ship commanders.

Above An Italian human torpedo of the type used in raids on British shipping.

Below A British two-man human torpedo gets underway on a mission into enemy waters.

Above The German battle-cruiser *Admiral Scheer*, the scourge of the Atlantic sea lanes.

Right Lieutenant Commander Günther Prien, commander of the German U-boat U-47, which sank the battleship *Royal Oak* in Scapa Flow.

Above The burnt-out hulk of the SS *San Demetrio,* manned by her gallant crew, limps into the Clyde after her epic adventure in the Atlantic.

Below A scene of devastation on board the *San Demetrio.*

Tugs bustle around the crippled tanker *Ohio* as she enters
Valletta harbour, Malta.

Above HMS *Hardy*, under the command of Captain Warburton-Lee, VC, took part in the Battle of Narvik.

Left Wrecked shipping in Narvik Bay after the attack by British warships in the early days of the war.

Above The German battleship *Bismarck,* pride of Hitler's navy.

Below The German heavy cruiser *Prinz Eugen, Bismarck's*
companion in the dash into the Atlantic.

Above HMS *Hood*. Britain's biggest battleship, was sent to the bottom by *Bismarck*'s guns.

Below The aircraft carrier *Ark Royal* after she had been struck a mortal blow by a German torpedo.

Above Lieutenant Commander Eugene Esmonde (second from left) led the daring Swordfish attack on the *Bismarck*.

Below A Fleet Air Arm Swordfish launches its torpedo.

Left Able Seaman William Savage, posthumously awarded the Victoria Cross for his courage at St Nazaire.

Below A flotilla of motor gun boats, of the type used in the St Nazaire raid, races into action.

Left Lieutenant Commander
S. H. Beattie, VC, captain
of HMS *Campbeltown*.

Below HMS *Campbeltown*.
firmly lodged in the caissons
of the Normandie dock just
before she blew up.

The German battleship *Tirpitz* at anchor in Altenfiord, Norway, ringed by anti-submarine nets.

The German battle-cruiser *Scharnhorst*.

An X-craft underway with its commander on deck by the conning tower.

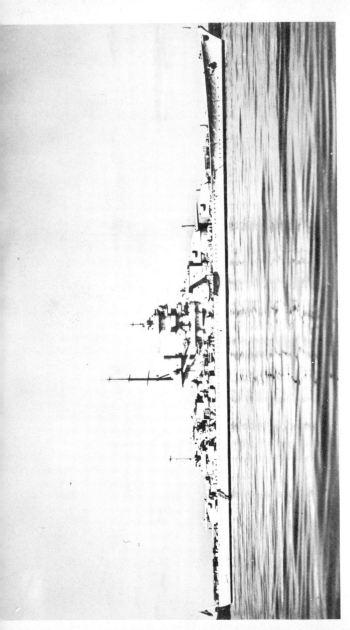

The *Gneisenau*.

World War came. All the channels into the Flow except the entrance channel were blocked by the scuttled ships and the British Fleet could shelter in the Flow with impunity—or so they thought . . .

The German navy had one burning desire—to penetrate the Flow's defences and strike at the British Fleet on its home ground while it was off guard. Twice it had been tried by submarines during the First World War and on both occasions the raids had failed with the loss of the crews of two German U-boats. But now the Germans were determined to realise their twenty-five-year-old dream and pull off an attack which was believed impossible. The British thought their Fleet was safe in the Scapa Flow basin and the Germans were happy to let them believe that—until one night in October 1939.

Almost by accident, a German U-boat had been drawn close to the entrances of Scapa Flow by the strong tides, giving her captain an opportunity of examining them and later reporting back to the German High Command. Immediately an aerial reconnaissance was ordered and German aircraft flew over the Orkneys photographing the Flow. The assembled photographs and information were studied closely by Kommodore Doenitz who pored over them endlessly, weighing up whether or not an attack could be made. Then at last he decided that it was indeed possible if a submarine sneaked into the Flow on the surface then made its attack on the Fleet from underwater at periscope depth. He wrote to his commander, Grand Admiral Raeder, telling him of the plan and then had the awesome task of finding a U-boat commander capable of leading such an operation. He had to select a man who possessed the vital qualities necessary for such a daring attack. This submariner had to be, above all, daring and courageous and one who would not crack under the strain of such a hazardous venture.

Doenitz knew all his submarine commanders personally. He knew their individual idiosyncrasies, their skills as captains and their ambitions. He was confident that not one of them would back out if asked to undertake the mission. The attack required skill at handling a submarine but the most essential quality was that of dash and daring. Doenitz was not looking for a man who had to sustain his courage for a great length of time. He wanted someone who would reach his peak performance quickly and need only hold it for a short time. He wanted a man hell-bent on personal glory; someone who was prepared to take risks to satisfy a lust for fame. Doenitz did not have to look long for his man. He was Lieutenant Commander Günther Prien, captain of the submarine U-47.

Prien was a die-hard Nazi who worshipped his Führer and a man whose lust for glory fired him with the dash and determination that Doenitz knew was vital to the operation. He was a small man and it was perhaps that that gave him an inner feeling of inferiority and goaded him into continually trying to be better than his comrades.

This outwardly self-confident man was ambitious and wildly temperamental not, one would have thought, the ideal person to command a submarine in which, on long voyages in cramped and enclosed spaces, a captain must be even-tempered and capable of keeping his head at all times. He was, however, just the man Doenitz wanted for the attack on Scapa Flow.

Prien's craving for distinction stemmed partially from his childhood. He came from a poor family and knew the pangs of hunger throughout his early days in his birthplace of Leipzig while the First World War ravaged Europe. Young Prien's desire was to escape the poverty and he was determined that he would make good and never have to live an impoverished existence again, so, with this thought in mind, he enlisted in the Merchant Marine. He was resolute in his purpose and allowed nothing to deviate him from his course. He studied hard and finally succeeded in gaining his Master's ticket but alas, because of the Depression, he was unable to get his own command.

Prien was dejected and despondent and it was while he was in that frame of mind that he began to show a serious interest in the wild oration of Adolf Hitler, the leader of the Nazi party, a political organisation which was fanatically anti-Jewish and hell-bent on the glorification of the Fatherland. To many Germans, Prien among them, Hitler was seen as a 'saviour', come to rescue Germany from her poverty-stricken abyss and return her to the pinnacle of power in Europe. Hitler blamed the Jews for Germany's downfall and his wild anti-Semitic speeches kindled the fires of hatred in the hearts of the German people . . . a hate which ultimately led to the murder of more than six million Jews at the hands of the Nazis.

More and more Germans throughout the country were joining the Nazi ranks and at last Prien saw his chance to attain his goal. He enrolled in the Nazi party and, as a sign of his total devotion to Hitler and his cause, Prien volunteered to work in a Nazi labour camp.

Hitler knew that if Germany was to rise to her former glory, she could only do so with powerful military forces to back her up. He was forbidden from building up his army, navy and air force by the terms of the German surrender at the end of the First World War, and he was limited to a comparatively small and virtually ineffective military force. Hitler, however, cared little for the surrender terms and he secretly set about building up a highly professional and powerful fighting force.

Prien knew of this and was quick to decide that his future lay with the navy and he enlisted as an ordinary seaman in the submarine service. Prien's ambition drove him on in the élite corps of submariners until a year before the outbreak of the Second World War when he took command of U-47. His rise through the ranks to reach his own command was meteoric and greatly impressed Doenitz. The Kommodore knew that this man, of all his submarine commanders, was best qualified for an attack on Scapa Flow. If any man could pull off this near-impossible mission, Prien could and so it was that, on 1 October 1939, he was summoned to Kommodore Doenitz's cabin on board the depot ship *Weichsel* in dock at Kiel.

Doenitz shook Prien's hand warmly and he and two other officers explained the mission. As they outlined the planned attack Prien became flushed with excitement. A great honour was being bestowed on him by his superiors in choosing him for this dangerous mission and, when he left the Kommodore's cabin, his head was buzzing. If he could succeed where others had failed he would be acclaimed throughout Germany. He was bursting to tell his comrades of his mission, to broadcast to the world that he, and he alone, had been chosen, but Doenitz had impressed upon him the need for utter secrecy so Prien had to keep the good news bottled-up inside himself.

There was never any question in his mind about whether or not he should take on the job but Doenitz had made it clear that, if Prien thought the mission too dangerous or hazardous, or if there was any reason whatsoever why he should not go, then all he had to do was decline and no one would think less of him. Prien, however, was determined to go through with it, no matter what the risks.

All through that night he pored over the maps, charts and aerial photographs of Scapa Flow, examining every entrance to it minutely, calculating tidal flows, depths and the best route he should take to ensure a safe passage into the British Fleet's base. At last he found a route; it was narrow and strewn with hazards but, according to his calculations, it was the opening which afforded the greatest chance of success. He chose the narrow stretch of water between the tiny island of Lamb Holm and the mainland of Orkney. The tides at that entrance were particularly fast and Prien realised he would require all the skill he could muster to manoeuvre his boat through the narrow passage. To make penetration even more difficult, the British had sunk three concrete-filled block ships, two of which lay diagonally across the narrow channel and the third slightly farther north of them. Between the northern block ship and the mainland was a very narrow channel but it was just deep enough to allow a submarine through into Scapa Flow itself.

Prien knew that the task set him would be difficult, if not almost impossible, and the following morning he visited Doenitz once more, this time to tell him formally that he would attempt the mission. Doenitz was delighted. The German navy was, at that time, out of favour with the Führer following the sinking of the *Athenia* but Doenitz saw this as an opportunity of gaining favour once more.

The date set for the attack was the night of 13/14 October when the moon was right and the flood-tide at its least vicious. And so it was that, only one week after Prien had agreed to the plan, U-47 left Germany en route for its objective, Scapa Flow.

The crew knew nothing of the real target and imagined they were outward bound on a routine patrol, slipping through the waves of the North Sea, diving only when they sighted a British trawler, lest they were spotted. Prien could not afford to jeopardise the mission by risking an engagement with the enemy. Even when he sighted British merchant ships which would have made worthy targets he stayed out of sight, much to the surprise of his crew, who knew him as a commander who would go to great lengths to sink an enemy.

On the morning of Friday the 13th, Prien gave the order to dive and U-47 slid beneath the waves until finally she rested on the sea-bed. It was then that he announced his plan to the crew.

'We are going into Scapa Flow tonight,' he said in a slow, matter-of-factual monotone. For a moment there was absolute silence as the crew absorbed the message, then the ship became alive with the sound of anxious and excited chatter.

Far from showing the slightest trepidation at the prospect of such a hazardous mission, the crew was charged with enthusiasm and keen to get on with the job but they were to have a long wait ahead of them. Prien planned to penetrate the narrow passage into the Flow at night and he decided to lie on the sea-bed until dark before proceeding.

All that day and into the evening the crew sat silent in the still submarine, none of them talking unnecessarily or moving around without good cause, to conserve oxygen which would be absolutely vital during the lengthy submerged attack.

Then, in the early evening, Prien stirred the ship

into action. At last they were on the move after a long and anxious wait on the bottom during which the pre-battle tension had mounted. But now, with work to do and the fray almost at hand, the tension eased and the U-boat rose through the sea to periscope depth.

'Up periscope,' Prien ordered and the long telescopic tube slid upwards from its well.

Prien's eager eyes peered into the 'scope as he turned it a full 360°, sweeping the seas in search of enemy ships lurking nearby but the rolling seas were empty. His lips parted in a half smile as he saw that the coast was clear.

'Surface!' he ordered and the submarine's bows broke water. Every move they made now, every decision Prien took, would have to be absolutely perfect, otherwise the whole mission would undoubtedly be a complete failure. They all knew it and concentrated their every effort in striving for perfection.

That night the moon was hidden by cloud as had been predicted, a point which Prien had calculated and banked on to cover him from observance, but there was one element which Prien could not have predicted—the Aurora Borealis, or Northern Lights as they were commonly called. These lights, caused by the sun's reflection off the polar ice-cap, danced and leapt across the sky, illuminating the sea—and U-47. Because of this phenomenon, Prien's chances of being spotted by an enemy ship or perhaps a keen-eyed look-out at Scapa Flow were much greater. However, in spite of this, the risk was worth taking. He was determined that nothing would stand in the way of success and U-47 cruised nearer to her goal.

All this time, Prien remained on the bridge with the salty spray from the boat's bows which cut through the water, splashing into his face. He was on edge, nervously anxious to get into the Flow and action, when he received a signal from Doenitz reporting that a reconnaissance flight over Scapa Flow earlier that day had shown units of the British Fleet, including five capital ships, at anchor there. If he could succeed in getting into Scapa Flow, Prien thought, the prizes would be good. Although he could not have known it at that time, the Fleet had sailed from Scapa Flow just a few hours earlier but there were still worthy targets left at anchor there.

At last he caught sight of the dumpy Orkney Islands ahead of his boat. The hour of trial was near at hand. But in an instant Prien's heart seemed to stop beating when he caught a glimpse of a ship riding the seas nearby.

'Dive! Dive!' he yelled and he scurried below closing the hatch as the boat plunged beneath the waves.

'Up 'scope!' he ordered breathlessly. Was the mission to be ruined by discovery at this crucial stage, he thought? He gripped the handles of the periscope and scanned the seas but there was no sign of the ship he thought he had sighted. Perhaps, in these last tension-filled moments before the attack, his eyes had been playing tricks on him. Relieved that the coast was clear, but not taking any chances, he remained underwater for half an hour before surfacing once more to begin the voyage through the narrow inlet to the Flow basin.

The outline of the islands took on a more definite shape as the submarine closed in on to its entry point, and soon the great lumpy islands miniaturised the U-boat.

It was shortly after midnight when the submarine nosed into the channel between Lamb Holm and the mainland and Prien and the crew could feel the tide grip the U-boat and force her towards the shore.

From the bridge, Prien gave short, crisp orders to the helmsman as he duelled with the tide. Ahead of him lay the block ships and the narrow passage through which he had to navigate his bulky craft. This was perhaps the most difficult and testing time in the whole operation.

The block ships and the islands were in darkness giving the scene an almost ghostly, frightening appearance. At any second the alarm could be raised and the mission become an abortive failure. But save for the hiss and swish of the sea as it cut over the boat's bows there was silence.

On she went into the narrowest part of the channel while only yards away to port lay a sunken block ship with the towering rocks of the mainland to starboard. The sea rushed even faster between these two obstacles catching the submarine and trying its hardest to turn the boat broadside on to the tidal race, but Prien's skilful handling of the U-boat kept her on course and she nosed between the sunken hulk and the rocks. She was almost through when Prien suddenly felt the boat shudder and scrape along the block ship. Luckily no damage was done and with a gasp of relief and a feeling of triumph in Prien's heart, the boat slid into Scapa Flow. She was into the British lair and already she had accomplished something no other German submarine had ever done before. But now Prien had to concentrate on seeking out and destroying British ships and he put U-47 on course for the middle of the Flow basin.

Still on the surface, U-47 sailed deeper into the Flow with its bubbling wake showing white and phosphorescent behind it. If nothing else was to betray her presence to the enemy, that streak of glowing white water would, but surprisingly no alarm was

73

raised and U-47 proceeded on her way without incident.

Prien searched the basin and found to his astonishment that the main Fleet anchorage was empty. He had not considered the possibility that the Fleet might not be there. What a terrible disappointment if, after all the dangers he and his crew had endured to get into the Flow, there were no targets!

In desperation, Prien swung the boat around in a wide arc, hugging the northern coastline of the basin. As he leant over the rim of the conning tower he peered into the darkness through powerful binoculars, then suddenly he gave a triumphant shout. Framed in the glasses was the towering black shape of a battleship, the *Royal Oak*, with a second ship anchored behind her. The second vessel was the *Pegasus* but, in the excitement, Prien thought she was the battle-cruiser *Repulse*.

Prien's orders came fast and furious. All tubes were ready as the submarine closed in for the attack and Prien ordered a spread of four torpedoes to be fired.

'Fire!' he shouted, and the boat shuddered as, one by one, the torpedoes shot out of their tubes and lanced through the water towards their target. Prien watched the bubbling trails of the torpedoes as they sped on then disappeared into the darkness. The seconds ticked by agonisingly slowly until Prien heard a low thump, but only one noise reached his ears. One of the torpedoes had struck *Royal Oak*'s anchor chain without dealing the ship a fatal blow, while the others had missed completely.

Prien could hardly believe that he had missed at such a short range and decided that the noise he had heard was a hit on the second ship. Furious, he swung the boat around and fired the stern torpedo at *Royal Oak* but again it was a miss.

74

'Prepare to reload!' he yelled at his crew, and he took the boat away from the *Royal Oak* while, for thirty long minutes the crew sweated and cursed until they had reloaded three torpedo tubes, right under the enemy's noses. Once again he lined up for the attack. This time, he swore, there would be no mistakes as he barked the order to release all three torpedoes.

From the bridge he watched the torpedo trails then his glasses swept up on to the target. An eternity seemed to pass before suddenly, just forward of the *Royal Oak*'s funnel, a vast column of water rose like a geyser from the sea almost to mast-height, followed by a great column of black smoke shot up into the air by the force of explosions. Then a huge tongue of orange flame lit up the whole area as a roar echoed across the water to Prien's ears. The ship's magazine had been hit and the *Royal Oak* was doomed.

On board the ship, chaos reigned as men were tossed into the sea when the ship heeled over. Below decks men drowned where they slept when thousands of tons of water rushed in, sweeping over them.

More explosions followed and reached Prien like music to his ears before the mast of the *Royal Oak* tilted sea-wards. Minutes later she settled in the water then disappeared amid a welter of sea and hissing steam. *Royal Oak* had sunk and with her went 780 men of her crew.

Prien was beside himself with joy at his success but his cries of joy were short-lived. He had yet to get his submarine out of Scapa Flow and back to Germany. Searchlights swept over the sea but none of their beams fell on U-47. Even when a destroyer ploughed through the waves towards them they remained undetected.

Once more Prien succeeded in negotiating the

passage between the block ship and the mainland and he slipped out to sea. The voyage back to Germany went without incident, and on 17 October U-47 arrived back at Kiel to be welcomed by Grand Admiral Raeder and Doenitz themselves with bands playing and the mighty ships of the German navy sounding their sirens in salute to Prien.

Prien and his crew were immediately flown to Berlin where they were presented to the Führer himself. If Hitler had had any doubts about the effectiveness of his navy in the past these doubts were swept away by Prien's daring act at Scapa Flow.

Lieutenant Commander Günther Prien's moment of crowning glory came when his Führer awarded him the Knight's Cross of the Iron Cross. He was a national hero and rode through the streets of Berlin in an open car drinking in the adulation shown by a hero-worshipping crowd.

Prien's penetration of the Scapa Flow defences and sinking must go down as one of the most daring and courageous submarine attacks in naval history, and without question he richly deserved the praise and honours that were lavished on him. However, the Royal Navy was to get its revenge some nineteen months later when Prien, attacking a British convoy in U-47, was killed by depth charges from HMS *Wolverine*. Germany had lost one of its most courageous mariners.

5

The Ships That Wouldn't Die

In 1940 Britain stood alone, an island people waging war with the military might of Nazi Germany. To survive and emerge victorious from that bitter conflict, Britain had to be supplied with food and munitions, petrol and aircraft parts, the bulk of which came from North America, across three thousand miles of ocean. It was vital that the sea route between America and Britain, the country's life-line along which these crucial materials flowed, be kept open and the job of ferrying these supplies across the Atlantic fell upon the British merchant marine.

The German High Command knew only too well that, without these supplies, Britain would be brought to her knees and they threw all their Atlantic sea power into the fight to sever that life-line with the United States. Groups of German U-boats scoured the ocean in 'wolf packs' hunting for British merchantmen, sneaking into the very heart of convoys of ships and unleashing torpedoes at the almost defenceless ships. Surface raiders like the battle-cruiser *Admiral Scheer* swept the ocean in search of prey and 'stood off' at long range, picking off the merchantmen with almost complete impunity.

The most sought-after prize of all for the U-boat commander or surface raider was the oil tanker laden with thousands of tons of oil or petrol to help quench the insatiable thirst of the British war machine. Apart from the ships which carried high-explosives, oil tankers were the most vulnerable and dangerous in which to go to sea in time of war. They were sitting ducks; slow, cumbersome and highly explosive. One well-aimed shell or torpedo could spell disaster for a tanker, as happened in all too many instances when a tanker blew-up into a hundred thousand bits leaving nothing but a towering pall of thick, black, oily smoke.

The crews of these ships were comprised of men to whom courage was second nature, always aware of their vulnerability and the thin thread by which their lives hung, but to a man determined to keep Britain's life-line intact.

The stories related in this chapter tell of just two ships and their crews who epitomised the courage and valour of these men of Britain's merchant marine.

* * * *

The Eagle Oil tanker *San Demetrio* sailed up the Atlantic coast of America as it made its way north from the Dutch East Indies to Canada, carrying a cargo of 11,000 tons of petrol in her tanks, destined for Britain. Every drop of petrol in her huge tanks was precious and the ship's master, Captain Waite, and his crew knew that the success of their voyage would mean that more British aircraft could fly their missions against Germany's Luftwaffe; that more ships could put to sea to do battle with the German Navy and that more factories throughout the length and breadth of Britain could carry on the job of manufacturing munitions for the Army's guns.

After an uneventful voyage up the coast *San Demetrio* arrived at Halifax, Nova Scotia, where she rendez-voused with thirty-six other merchant ships to form a convoy for the Atlantic crossing. Their only escort for the crossing was to be the armed merchant-cruiser *Jervis Bay*, under the command of Captain E. S. F. Fegan RN.

On 28 October, the thirty-seven merchant ships formed up into a nine-column convoy, with *San Demetrio* leading the eighth column, and headed out into the Atlantic. Tension mounted as the ships crept slowly out to sea and into the hunting ground of the German U-boats and surface raiders.

San Demetrio was four days out of Halifax when engine trouble struck and she had to drop out of the convoy while the ship's engineers busied themselves sorting out the trouble. They worked as fast as they could with the *San Demetrio* rolling in the gathering Atlantic swell. On the bridge, lookouts watched as the convoy disappeared over the horizon. They were alone and easy prey for any German marauders who might be at hand.

It took sixteen hours of arduous work for the engineers to get the engines thumping into life once more and every man on board breathed a sigh of relief when the ship got underway once more.

With her engines throbbing, the tanker raced as best she could to join up with the convoy but it took almost seven long tension-filled days before she was able to take her place in the dubious sanctuary of the almost defenceless fleet of ships.

The eager eyes of the lookouts of the watch scoured the horizon for the tell-tale signs of enemy ships and swept across the rolling waves for the sight of a U-boat's periscope while the convoy sailed ponderously on. Meanwhile the crew of the *San Demetrio* went about their tasks, none of them showing the ever-present feeling of apprehension that dwelt within all sailors who plied these troubled seas. Two young teenage boys, Apprentice Jones and Cadet Housden, were to show that before twenty-four hours had passed they could match the courage and determination of even the hardiest old salt, and they went about their duties with a confidence seldom seen in landborne boys of their age.

The morning of 5 November broke with ominous grey clouds hanging over a rolling green sea. It was icy cold and the men on watch muffled themselves against the biting wind and blew into their cupped hands to restore some warmth to their stiffening fingers.

The dull day wore on until, around 4·30 pm, Second Officer Hawkins was striding aft along the deck to where the ship's only gun was situated. His trained eye automatically swept the horizon until he stopped dead in his tracks. There was something out there. What it was he could not immediately discern but his eye fixed on what looked like a puff of smoke on the horizon. Gradually the hazy shape became clearer until he was left in no doubt what it was—the topmast of a warship heading in their direction. No British or Allied ships were known to be in that area and only one conclusion could be drawn—it was German.

As if to confirm his suspicions, the ear-piercing whine of heavy shells arcing through the sky towards them, built into a deafening crescendo over the steady throbbing of their engines and the whistling of the wind. A split second later the shells fell among the convoy sending great plumes of sea shooting into the air as they exploded. Instantly, red and green rockets burst into the sky from the Commodore's flagship, the SS *Cornish City*. This was the sign to scatter and the convoy broke up, with ships veering off in different directions and shattering the German's compact target. But alas the evasive action was not to save the *San Demetrio* from the wrath of the German's guns. A second salvo screeched through the air and a shell tore into the ship's forehold causing serious damage.

Meanwhile, Captain Fogarty Fegan in *Jervis Bay* ordered his ship hard-to-port towards the battle-cruiser which was pounding down on his scattered convoy. With engines at full power, *Jervis Bay* sliced its way through the rolling waves towards the oncoming enemy in a bid to draw its fire and allow the merchant ships to escape the hail of shells that rained down on them.

Fegan's ruse worked but it brought all of the battle-cruiser's guns to bear on it. *Jervis Bay* was lashed with shells and was soon on fire but Fegan pressed relentlessly on. Still the merciless barrage of shells pounded into the merchant-cruiser which had no armour plating and only short-range six-inch guns with which to reply to the German's heavy guns. Fegan could not have chosen a more formidable adversary with which to do battle. The German ship was none other than the battle-cruiser *Admiral Scheer*, one of the most powerful ships afloat.

For three hours the battle between these two ships raged until, blazing and torn to pieces by the weight of the enemy's fire, the *Jervis Bay* sank. Fegan had sacrificed his ship and his crew so that the convoy might escape under cover of smoke. He was later posthumously awarded the Victoria Cross.

But while the battle between the *Admiral Scheer* and the *Jervis Bay* had been fought the *San Demetrio* had slipped away out of range. Captain Waite was posed with a difficult decision. Should he head towards home unprotected through dangerous waters with the vital cargo he carried, or should he head back to Newfoundland and wait for another convoy? He consulted his officers and they agreed that they should head for home, come what may. With that decision taken Waite set course for home. Had he but known it then, he was sailing into danger.

Kapitan zur See Theodor Krancke, the commander of the *Admiral Scheer*, had foreseen that some of the convoy of ships would make a bid to reach Britain and he steamed on a course to intercept them. Half an hour after Waite's change of course, the darkness through which the merchantman now sailed became a blaze of light as star shells burst overhead. They had been found and a split second later came the roar of the *Admiral Scheer*'s guns. The huge black mass of the German raider glowed with orange flashes as the guns opened up at almost point blank range. The *San Demetrio* didn't stand a chance. First came a salvo of shells which straddled the tanker then a second smashed into the superstructure. White hot pieces of jagged metal flashed through the air faster than the speed of sound while fires broke out around the ship. She was doomed.

'Stop all engines!' Waite ordered. 'Abandon ship!'

Men dashed about the ship and lowered the lifeboats. Miraculously, all but three of the ship's crew, a young able seaman and two wireless operators who had been killed, managed to scramble into the lifeboats. Then, as the men put their backs into heaving at the oars, the *Admiral Scheer* fired another salvo and the shells found their mark. Now the entire ship was a raging inferno belching fire and thick, black smoke. At any second the whole ship could explode in a great ball of flame which would engulf the survivors as they rowed with all their strength.

Yet more shells were fired at the ship, adding to the damage. The bridge was shattered beyond recognition and a shell ripped a gaping hole in her port bow. It was a sorrowful sight and one that tugged at the hearts of the crewmen who watched her burn. Luckily for them *San Demetrio* did not explode, even when the *Admiral Scheer* continued to fire into her.

The three lifeboats from the *San Demetrio* drifted off into the night and became separated from each other. The Number One lifeboat was under the command of Second Officer Hawkins, the man who had originally sighted the *Scheer* on the horizon before her disastrous attack. Into his lifeboat were crammed sixteen men who were to take part in what has now become one of the epic adventures of merchant marine history. The other two boats were to drift for some time before they were eventually found and the survivors picked up and taken safely back to Canada. For the men in the Number One lifeboat their ordeal was just beginning.

The heavy seas crashed over the small boat, drenching everyone in it and chilling them to the bones. Soaked through to the skin, with the icy wind biting into their bodies, their strength was soon sapped away. To add to their misery, the continual tossing of the boat on the waves played havoc with their stomachs and all of them were violently sea-sick.

But in spite of their waning strength, they fought to keep the boat's head into the wind to prevent it from being swamped completely by the towering waves. The storm continued unabated all through the night, relentlessly trying its best to capsize the boat and toss its occupants into the freezing cold sea.

When dawn came, their worst fears were realised. They were alone in an empty sea with no sign of help on the deserted horizon. Their chances of survival seemed remote. But then, when it had been light for almost two hours, one of them caught sight of a ship. Hopes rose quickly only to be dashed when the ship passed on out of sight, over the horizon.

Not long after, another ship was sighted. Luck must be with them, they thought, and they put all their renewed strength into pulling on the oars. But as they drew closer, there seemed to be something very familiar about the ship. They couldn't believe their eyes and they all gazed open-mouthed at the ship . . . it was the *San Demetrio*!

The huge tanker was still ablaze and clouds of thick, black smoke continued to belch out of her. She was well down at the head with tons of water sweeping into her as each towering wave engulfed her bows. But the most startling thing of all was that she was still afloat!

The decision that now faced the men in the boat was whether or not to re-board her. The lifeboat in which they were sailing was built of steel and everyone on-board knew only too well that one spark from her as she drew alongside the tanker might well set light to the petrol that was pouring from her tanks and floating on top of the water surrounding the ship. They weighed up the the situation. They could stay in their lifeboat and probably freeze to death, die of exposure or drown. They could go on board the *San Demetrio* and at least have some shelter from the howling gale that tossed them about the sea but face the possibility of being blown sky-high if the petrol went up.

Keeping the tiny lifeboat as best they could on the weather side of the ship the men discussed the alternatives throughout the night and decided that, if she was still with them in the morning, they would make an attempt to board her. Then they got down to sleep as best they could under the terrible weather conditions that prevailed.

When morning came the *San Demetrio* made up their minds for them. It had disappeared during the night. That, they thought, was that and what seemed like their only chance of survival had gone. But fire or not, they all wished that they had made an attempt to board her. Anything, they thought, was preferable to the living hell they were going through, tossing about on the waves of a cruel and tempestuous sea.

Weary, sea-sick and with their strength almost completely gone from their tired bodies they almost gave up hope of reaching safety. But then one of the crew gave a yell.

'There she is! It's her!'

At first everyone thought he was dreaming but sure enough she was there and drifting away from them. With renewed heart they raised the sail and set course for the still burning tanker. As the others rowed with all their strength, two of the seamen, MacNeil and McLennan, both of them hardy seamen from the Scottish island of Barra, set about sailing the boat through the mighty waves. They were well used to sailing boats in bad seas as both of them had been fishermen in wild waters around their native Hebrides. Slowly but surely the boat gained on the drifting tanker and at last they reached her stern where they found that the remnants of a Jacobs ladder which had been used when they abandoned ship still hung over the stern. There was no hesitating now about boarding her. They draped some blankets over the boat's gunwales to lessen the chance of sparks when the two craft touched, then one of the seamen, Oswald Preston, a Canadian known as 'Yank', scaled the ladder with a painter and secured the lifeboat. One by one they struggled aboard in spite of their condition, all except Stoker Boyle who had to be hoisted aboard because he already had many broken ribs as a result of his jumping into the lifeboat when they first abandoned ship.

At last they were all on board and they surveyed the scene. It was one of complete devastation. The main deck was buckled, twisted and punctured with holes out of which petrol spurted with every roll of the ship. The slightest spark and they and the ship would almost certainly disappear without a trace.

The *San Demetrio* was nothing short of a floating wreck. The navigation bridge was shattered, destroyed by a shell, and the metal in the wheel-house and chart room was still white hot; the accommodation amidships was burnt out and the whole of the port side aft was a smoking ruin. With the exception of the cabins on the starboard side aft, all of them had been completely gutted. Every piece of navigational equipment had been destroyed as well as the radio and steering gear. But in spite of all this damage and the fires onboard, the twisted and mangled hulk remained afloat. The prospect of being able to stay safely onboard the ship seemed slim but they were soon to be left with little choice when their lifeboat broke loose and disappeared in the swirling sea. That left them with only a twelve-foot-long Shetland dinghy which wouldn't stand a chance of riding out an Atlantic gale. So there they were and, like it or not, there they would have to stay.

The most immediate danger lay in the fires spreading and they set about the task of extinguishing them by the painfully slow and laborious method of hand by hand bucket parties while Chief Engineer Pollard, Third Engineer Willey, Store-man Davies and Stoker Boyle undertook the awesome task of getting the engines in working order. They had all decided that they had but one hope of survival left—to get the ship underway and sail home!

In spite of their injuries and pitiful state of health, all

the men, including the boys, set about their allotted tasks with enthusiasm. Young Jones had a lip swollen to an enormous size which caused him continuous and agonising pain but he did his bit along with the others.

By the first afternoon, they had, by an amazing piece of ingenuity, repaired the electricity generator and were able to bring the hoses into action and also pump the thousands of gallons of water out of the engine room. It was not, however, until the following morning that they finally managed to extinguish all the fires. One of them found some tea stowed in a cabin and they had the most enjoyable brew up any of them had ever had. All during that morning they plugged the holes in the deck with wood and cotton waste. With that done they turned their attentions to working out how they were to steer the ship, that is providing they managed to get it underway. At last they succeeded in devising a reasonably effective steering gear out of the auxiliary steering gear in the after part of the ship. But with that done they still had to work out a system of signals from the deck to the engine room. They arranged a series of lights and devised a code which indicated whether the ship was to go 'ahead', astern or stop.

Then the great moment came when Chief Engineer Pollard tested his engines. Astonishingly they ran sweetly and the throb of the ship came like music to the crew's ears. Hawkins signalled 'ahead' from the deck and the *San Demetrio* moved slowly through the water. Miraculously, they were underway.

With all the navigational equipment destroyed, navigation by conventional means was virtually impossible and it was by almost pure guesswork that Hawkins set course for home while four men took turns at the helm.

Their troubles were far from over though. The weather worsened and the sea crashed over the ship's deck, wrenching out the improvised plugs and allowing petrol to spill out, adding to the danger of more fire. In addition the ship was once more well down at the head and Hawkins decided that to help keep her head up, he would transfer the petrol from the forward tank to the one amidships. It was a long and dangerous task but eventually they succeeded and the ship ploughed on through the water at a steady nine knots.

When Sunday came Hawkins held a short service of Thanksgiving for their deliverance from almost certain death.

By the following Wednesday the storm had abated and Hawkins reckoned that, if his calculations had been correct, they must make a landfall soon. And indeed, shortly after mid-day on that very day land was sighted. They had no idea which country they were approaching but they soon discovered that it was southern Ireland when naval launches raced out to meet them. They had done it. Against terrible odds they had pulled off the impossible.

But having come that far on their own they were determined to continue their voyage under their own steam and on 15 November the *San Demetrio* sailed triumphantly up the River Clyde.

Without charts, compass or proper steering gear, they had accomplished a miracle of damage control which which would have taxed the ingenuity of men who had proper tools and equipment and brought their ship home with their much needed cargo of petrol.

For his masterful handling of the ship, Second Officer Hawkins was decorated with the Order of the British Empire along with others of the ship's crew who received decorations.

The *San Demetrio* was, alas, not to see the end of the war. After a refit on the Clyde, she went back into service but was sunk off the American coast when she was attacked by a German U-boat.

*   *   *   *

During the Second World War, the tiny island of Malta situated in the Mediterranean Sea was of vital strategic importance to the Allies, not only for their war against the German and Italian armies in the North African desert but for the eventual invasion of Sicily and the Italian mainland. Like Britain, Malta, which had taken the most incredible pounding from German and Italian bombers based in Italy, had to be supplied with the vital materials of war and, like Britain, the most important of these was oil. There was but one way to get that vital liquid to the beleaguered island and that was by sea. But, unlike the Atlantic convoys, the Malta convoys were harassed by yet another menace, enemy aircraft. Convoys passing through the blue Mediterranean were within range of German and Italian bombers and fighters as well as being within striking distance of the Italian fleet and the U-boat packs. The Maltese people stood up resolutely against the day and night fighter and bomber attacks by the Axis air forces but they could not defend themselves without fighter planes and fuel for their engines. The task of delivering a consignment of fuel fell upon one of the *San Demetrio*'s sister ships, the *Ohio*.

Early in August 1942, the 14,000 ton oil tanker *Ohio* took on 13,000 tons of petroleum products and made ready to sail from the Clyde. She had been specially chosen for the task because she was the fastest tanker in the fleet and, in the voyage through the Mediterranean, speed was to be of the essence.

Every member of the crew had been hand picked. The master, Captain Mason, was the youngest captain in the fleet and the Chief Engineer, Mr Wyld, was one of the most experienced in the business. Besides the normal working crew, a special twenty-three man gun crew was taken onboard. When all was ship-shape the *Ohio* sailed and joined the remainder of the convoy which was to force its way through to Malta. Such was the importance of their mission, that a host of Royal Navy vessels was to escort *Ohio* and the other merchant ships in the convoy. Among these were the battleships *Nelson* and *Rodney*, the aircraft carriers *Indomitable*, *Victorious*, *Eagle* and *Furious*, which carried replacement fighter aircraft for Malta, the cruisers *Sirius*, *Charybdis*, *Phoebe*, *Kenya*, *Manchester*, *Nigeria* and *Cairo*, along with thirty-two destroyers, one of the biggest convoys ever to put to sea.

The powerful fleet of ships slipped through the Straits of Gibraltar under cover of darkness on the night of 8/9 August 1942, but as they ploughed on through the calm Mediterranean seas, the German and Italian air and sea forces were waiting for them.

Forty-eight hours passed without sight of the enemy then she struck just as surely as a hammer blow. A great column of water erupted out of the sea beside the aircraft carrier *Eagle* along with a series of dull explosions. A U-boat had slipped in through the net of destroyers and fired a salvo of torpedoes. Within minutes the *Eagle* was listing, the aircraft on her deck sliding off the crazily-angled deck and into the sea. In only seven minutes she turned over with smoke and steam belching from her and slid beneath the boiling sea and vanished. All that remained of the carrier was a huge stain of oil on the surface and the bobbing heads of the survivors of her crew. The enemy had struck its first deadly blow.

Almost unable to believe what they had witnessed the thousands of sailors onboard the ships returned to their tasks and the convoy pressed on over the sparkling sea. That afternoon, the ominous drone of approaching bombers was heard. The battle royal was about to begin.

Stuka dive-bombers hurtled down out of the sky raining bombs on to the ships as they carved their way through the sea and suddenly every gun opened up at the screaming planes. The sky was instantly peppered with puffs of smoke as anti-aircraft shells burst, scattering their white-hot metal about the sky. The agonising din of battle tortured the ears of the men on the ships as the aircraft's sirens wailed heralding an attack. British fighters swept into the air from the carriers and their guns took their toll of the diving enemy planes.

Ships weaved crazy courses in a bid to fox the German pilots and avoid their bombs while the fighters and guns blasted away at the bombers knocking thirty-nine of them out of the sky.

The German pilots had special instructions to pay particular attention to one ship in the convoy—the *Ohio*—and time after time bombs plummetted into the water only feet away from the tanker. She was soon drenched with tons of blue sea but she plodded relentlessly on amid the onslaught and remained unscathed.

When evening came the battle grew in a furious crescendo, intensifying almost beyond belief. The Germans were throwing every aircraft they had into the air in a frantic bid to halt the convoy but, in spite of losses, the fleet of ships sailed resolutely on.

The following day dawned and brought with it another determined attack with the ships pumping lead into the sky in a furious barrage. Asdic sets on the escorting destroyers pinged betraying the presence of submarines and exploding depth charges transformed the sea into a boiling cauldron of water.

Evening came and still the enemy had failed to secure a hit on the most important target of all, the *Ohio*. But Captain Mason's luck was not to last for much longer. When dusk came the *Ohio* was shaken by a violent explosion. A torpedo had struck her, jolting the ship, shattering the steering gear and wrecking all the communication lines with the engine room and the after end of the ship. The torpedo had blasted an enormous hole in the main deck and tank lids were wrenched open and buckled by the force of the explosion. Still the bombers swept down on the ship with renewed determination now that a hit had been scored while, on the decks, the fire parties fought to extinguish the spreading flames. As bomber after bomber raced in to attack, the crews manning the ship's Bofors and Oerlikon guns opened up at them sending up a curtain of fire.

The engines had stopped but deep down in the engine room Chief Engineer Wyld and his men battled heroically to get them turning once more. Now that she was stopped, *Ohio* was sitting alone in the Mediterranean, the convoy having to press on without her. She was a perfect target for prowling U-boats almost motionless in the water but, mercifully, Wyld succeeded in getting the engines going once more and she got underway, managing to rejoin the convoy the following morning. But no sooner had she done so than another attack began. It seemed as if every enemy aircraft was hell-bent on the destruction of the *Ohio* for wave after wave of them thundered in on her, straddling her with bombs. The deck was now a scene of absolute chaos with wreckage strewn all over it and the gaping hole in her side letting in water. Then in a flash a Stuka swept in and crashed into the foredeck, breaking up and bursting into flames. Not long after that, two sticks of bombs hit the water on either side of the ship and actually lifted her clear out of the water. In the attack her electric fuel pumps were put out of commission and had to be repaired. But by now the crippled tanker could barely make four knots as she struggled through the water.

More aircraft attacked but many of them were thwarted in their attempts to deliver the final, killing blow by the accurate fire from *Ohio*'s guns. Then disaster struck. First her port boiler blew only to be followed seconds later by her starboard boiler blowing.

Captain Mason was left now with no alternative but to ask for a tow from one of the destroyers but try as they might, and they struggled for almost six hours, they could not secure the tow rope. Then it came. The whistle of a bomb followed by a sickening explosion as it blew up the boiler room, wrecking it completely.

But the end of the ordeal was at last in sight when British Beaufighter aircraft roared overhead flying protective cover while Spitfire fighters wheeled about the sky, giving the tanker crew some reassurance. But she had still to get to Valletta Harbour and unload her cargo.

All through the night the crew tried to fix a tow line but without success and when morning came it brought with it more bombers intent on destroying the stricken ship. One bomb carried away the ship's rudder and holed the stern. At last, on the sixth morning of their

Mediterranean ordeal, with a destroyer on each side of her and one ahead, she got underway but by then she was sinking fast at the stern and water was gushing into her at the rate of six inches an hour. While the crew fought to keep the ship afloat, the gunners warded off more and more air attacks until at dusk that night the crew caught sight of Malta and tugs raced out to meet her and take her on the last lap of her voyage.

On Saturday, 15 August, the *Ohio* entered Valletta harbour only two days late. She was all but a floating wreck but she had brought her valuable cargo of oil. On the bridge, Captain Mason watched as bands on the dockside played and thousands of people cheered the gallant crew. Had it not been for the perseverance and determination of Mason and his crew Malta might not have survived to play the vital role it did in the remainder of the war.

For his courage and that of his crew, Captain Mason was awarded the George Cross and Chief Engineer Wyld became one of the first men in the merchant marine to be awarded the Distinguished Service Order. Amongst the remainder of the officers and crew five Distinguished Service Crosses and seven Distinguished Service Medals were awarded.

To the men of the Merchant Marine, Britain owes an everlasting debt of gratitude.

6

The Battle of Narvik

Hitler began his conquest of Norway in April 1940 when he invaded the country with air and sea-borne forces, sweeping in on the vital Norwegian sea ports. The Führer cared nothing for Norway's neutrality. His sole concern was to ensure the constant supply of iron-ore to his weapon factories in Germany and it was from Norway that the bulk of his supply came. Although neutral, Norway was by nature more closely allied to Britain than Germany and, therefore, more likely to hinder him in his North Sea operations. In addition, that stretch of land with its rugged coastline might provide him with an ideal launching pad for a future invasion of Britain. All these were good reasons why Hitler felt that he must command Norway.

While paratroopers landed from squadrons of air transport planes at strategic points, units of the German navy, including navy destroyers, swept in on the ports, many of which were located deep in the fiords along the coast. It was at one of these ports, far into a fiord, where one of the most famous of all the sea battles of World War II was fought. The Battle of Narvik was to mark indelibly in the history pages the courage of Britain's destroyer crews.

On the night of 9 April, German destroyers were busily unloading their cargoes of soldiers to occupy the port at Narvik but, in spite of their success in overcoming the opposition at the port, they were in a particularly dangerous position for they could, quite easily, remain bottled-up in the fiord with their escape route to the sea blockaded by ships of the Royal Navy on station at the mouth of the fiord. It was crucial to the German destroyers that they refuel as quickly as possible and get out of the fiord before the Royal Navy had a chance to seal their passage to the sea. Speed was essential and time was running out fast. Their chances of making good their escape were further hampered because all the destroyers were short of fuel and with only one refuelling ship available they could take on fuel only two at a time, and this was a painfully slow business. It seemed as if the destroyers would be delayed for a whole day before they could make their dash for the sea. But while the Germans worked frantically to refuel, the Royal Navy was already on the advance.

The weather was bad, with heavy snow-storms adding a deeper white mantle to the snow covered cliffs that rose sheer from the fiord's edge. Through this howling, white storm five British destroyers, *Hardy, Hotspur, Hunter, Havoc* and *Hostile*, carved a path up the fiord. The flotilla was under the command of Captain Warburton-Lee, a seasoned sailor noted for his courage and daring. He knew that the enemy had landed troops at Narvik but he had no idea how many ships were still there. Before he would put his head in the noose, he was determined to find out just what sort of opposition he would be up against. So he sent a party ashore to find out at the pilot station located at Tranöy. Luckily the Norwegians were only too anxious to help, and they warned that at least six German destroyers and a U-boat had been sighted sailing up the fiord to Narvik. They also added that the port itself was by then heavily defended by the Germans, and that it would take a force considerably larger than Warburton-Lee's to dislodge them. The gallant captain, however, was not to be detracted from his purpose. He had one vital factor on his side, even if he were to face a larger force, and that was the element of surprise.

Warburton-Lee pondered for a while on how he should make his attack, then made a signal to the Admiralty:

'Intend attacking at dawn, high water.'

With his mind made up he led his ships seawards to a point where he would wait until the time was right for the attack. As luck would have it, his convoy of warships was sighted by an enemy submarine, the U-51, and the U-boat commander radioed the Narvik commander that he had seen a flotilla heading *out to sea*. Nothing could have suited Warburton-Lee better, for the commander at Narvik now thought that the destroyers would not be attacking; Kommodore Bonte, the German commander, heaved a sigh of relief.

At the appointed hour, Warburton-Lee's destroyers began their journey up the fiord into a fierce blizzard of snow, nosing their way between the mountainous cliffs which rose sharply hundreds of feet on either side of them. The journey was fraught with hazards and the slightest error in navigation could spell disaster—even before the battle had begun. But the foul weather did have an advantage in that it acted as a cloak for the advancing flotilla and added to their chances of a surprise attack on the German ships. The convoy, led by Warburton-Lee in *Hardy*, almost came to grief when a look-out spotted the white wall of a cliff dead ahead. It was only by the swift action of the helmsman that they averted disaster.

On they went, nearing their objective, as the grey light of dawn gave a ghostly appearance to the now mist-bound fiord. At last daylight came and they emerged from the mist. On board each of the British ships every man was at battle stations eagerly awaiting the call to action, while Narvik was wakening from its sleep. The port was quiet save for the sound of the gulls screeching over the ships lying at anchor. But in an instant the scene of tranquillity was transformed into a raging battle-field as the massed guns of the five destroyers flamed into action. The din of battle shook the entire fiord and sent great clumps of snow tumbling down off the steep rises into the water, as shells thudded into the stationary ships and exploded in jagged balls of orange fire. Torpedoes slid from their tubes with a hiss and plunged into the water to race to their targets, leaving a bubbling trail behind them.

A 'tin fish' slammed into the destroyer *Heidkamp* and exploded in her magazine, ripping the guts out of the ship and killing almost everyone aboard, including Kommodore Bonte. Then the destroyer *Schmitt* took the full force of a torpedo which lifted her out of the water breaking her in two. Dazed German guns crews stumbled along their decks unable to believe what was happening, many of them falling victim to the storm of shells that rained down on them.

The destroyer *Roeder* was pounded by shells which set her alight, enveloping the ship in flame, and half-crazed seamen leapt from her deck into the ice-cold water only to killed by the lethal shock-waves reverberating through the water from exploding shells. Chaos reigned throughout the harbour as Warburton-Lee's flotilla mercilessly kept up its unremitting barrage of fire.

Merchant ships anchored in the harbour did not escape the attack and several were sunk or severely damaged. The hell of the battle continued to rock the port and still the Germans had not come to their senses and taken any defensive action. Then in a gallant attempt to reply to the onslaught, a salvo of torpedoes was fired from the burning *Roeder*, but these missed the British ships completely. More shore batteries opened up, some of which were instantly silenced by concentrated fire from the British ships.

Warburton-Lee thought the time right to withdraw before the German guns found their range and, under under cover of smoke, the five destroyers turned away from the scene of devastation. Five of the six German destroyers which the Norwegians had told them were at Narvik had been dealt with but Warburton-Lee was still not satisfied. He wanted yet another crack at them just to make sure, and he launched another attack. Sailing in line-ahead, the destroyers raced into the harbour mouth, unleashing more torpedoes, then they retreated hurriedly away from the now intensive German fire.

The destroyers churned up the water as they headed seawards with their job complete. Warburton-Lee had every reason to feel pleased at the success of his journey up the fiord. But that feeling of elation was soon to be dashed when ahead of him he saw three more German destroyers racing towards the flotilla. The Norwegians had been wrong in their estimation of the German strength. Here were three ships which had been anchored in a nearby offshoot of the main fiord.

The situation was dangerous to say the least. The German ships had a greater fire-power than the British destroyers and were, indeed, larger but they did not have the speed of Warburton-Lee's flotilla. Discretion at that point was unquestionably the better part of valour and Warburton-Lee led his ships off at top speed with the Germans in hot pursuit. He might well have made it to the sea unscathed had it not been for the appearance of yet another two German destroyers ahead of the fleeing flotilla. Now they were trapped between two enemy forces which they knew would show them no mercy, and the roar of guns resounded from both of the German forces.

Warburton-Lee, with a typical touch of bravado, hoisted the signal Nelson himself had used so often in battle, 'Engage the enemy more closely'.

No sooner had the signal flags unfurled than the bridge of the *Hardy* was shattered by a direct hit. Warburton-Lee was fatally wounded while around him lay dead and injured men. Paymaster-Lieutenant Stanning was amongst those injured but he dragged himself off the bridge floor and surveyed the carnage about him. He himself had been badly injured in the leg, but his main concern was for the ship which was steering a crazy course along the fiord. He had to do something—and quickly—but what?

The Paymaster, whose job on board ship was to decipher codes and take care of administrative duties, was not expected to carry out—and indeed was not trained for—executive duties. But Stanning, realising what a perilous position his ship was in, had to make the best of it. He had seen enough of the ship's working to realise that the ship was out of control, and he knew that the only way to save her was to get to the steering wheel and get her on as safe a course as possible.

Dragging his limp, aching leg, he made his way painfully down the steps to the wheelhouse below the bridge and grabbed the wheel from the limp hands of the dead coxswain, and steered the ship as best he could down the fiord until, thankfully, a seaman arrived to take over from him.

More shells from the German ships hammered

down on the *Hardy* and Stanning saw that the ship was doomed. He took the sensible course of action and ordered that the ship be run aground on the rocky bank of the fiord to give the crew a chance of surviving the attack. Had he not done so, the destroyer would undoubtedly have been pounded to a wreck by the enemy shells.

As the helmsman wound the wheel hard over, the ship turned and ground on to the rocks. She was well and truly beached but between the crew and the shore lay 200 yards of freezing water. The *Hardy* was no place to be, and the freezing water was preferable to the fiery hell on board the ship, and the few survivors struggled ashore, some of them rescuing their shipmates, then returning to the ill-fated *Hardy* to look for more suvivors. Among those taken to the shore was Warburton-Lee. But although he reached the snowy shore alive, he died later of his wounds.

While the survivors of the *Hardy* fought their way ashore, the *Hunter* took the full force of the enemy fire and almost instantly became a fiery tomb for the crew. The ship swerved crazily and was hit broadsides by the *Hotspur* which was travelling at full speed. The two ships were locked together and still the German guns rained shells down on them. But at last, *Hotspur*, by now a mangled wreck but still floating, managed to disengage herself, while the two remaining British destroyers, *Hostile* and *Havoc* swept past her, heading seawards.

Hotspur got up as much power as she could and headed after the two undamaged destroyers. Luck must have been with her because the pursuing German ships were running desperately short of fuel and could not keep up the chase. Miraculously, the three remaining ships of the British destroyer flotilla escaped the wrath of the German guns. The *Hardy* and the *Hunter* were lost, but at the cost of these two ships, the German navy had suffered considerable damage.

Of the ten German destroyers two of them, the *Schmitt* and the *Heidkamp*, had been sunk, three of them, the *Arnim, Roeder* and *Thiele*, were totally out of action, and one other, the *Künne*, was severely damaged. Only three German destroyers, the *Köllner, Zenker* and *Giese*, were undamaged, but they had already expended most of their ammunition. But fate was to make matters even worse for them . . .

As the three British destroyers sailed out of the fiord, they spotted a German merchant ship, the *Rauenfels*, ploughing through the sea into the fiord, obviously heading for Narvik. Whatever her cargo, she merited attack and was shelled by *Hostile* and *Havoc* after the crew had abandoned ship. The *Rauenfels* must have been loaded to the gunwale with ammunition for, a few minutes later, she exploded in a great ball of fire. The German destroyers were to be denied the vital shells to feed their guns, and the sinking of that ship was to play a crucial part in the battle that was to follow. The first Battle of Narvik was over, but the Royal Navy was by no means finished with the destroyers that lay at Narvik—they were determined to wipe out the entire German destroyer force at the port.

On 12 April two squadrons of Swordfish aircraft took off from the aircraft-carrier *Furious* in a bid to deliver the final, fatal blow to the German destroyers. The first squadron actually reached the target, having flown through indescribably bad weather, only to have their bombs miss the targets completely. The fact that the raid was a failure can in no way be a reflection on the skill of the pilots for their aircraft were designed as torpedo-bombers and not dive-bombers.

The second squadron to launch an attack could not find Narvik at all because of the bad weather, and had to return to the *Furious* with their bomb-loads.

It seemed that there was but one way to destroy the German ships at Narvik and that was to mount another sea-borne attack. A formidable force of British warships was got together for the raid. Under the command of Admiral Whitworth, in the battleship *Warspite*, were four Tribal Class destroyers, *Cossack, Bedouin, Eskimo* and *Punjabi*, and five smaller destroyers, *Icarus, Foxhound, Forester, Hero* and *Kimberley*. On the afternoon of the 13th, Whitworth's armada made its way into the fiord towards its objective—Narvik.

But as the British ships sliced through the passage to their target, news reached the Germans of their approach, and Captain Bey, the new German commander, laid a trap for the British naval force. His ambush, however, was to prove fruitless because the *Warspite* launched its Swordfish reconnaissance float-plane, which soared over the fiord warning the British of the menace that lay in wait for them.

Then, as the Swordfish wheeled round to return to *Warspite*, the crew spotted a surfaced submarine lying in a fiord, waiting for the oncoming British ships. The pilot, Petty Officer Price, dropped the nose of his aircraft and shot down towards the U-boat. As he did so, his finger jabbed the bomb release button and a cluster of bombs hurtled towards the submarine. The missiles whistled through the air, then smashed into the submarine, exploding and sending her to the bottom. One less obstacle lay in the path of Whitworth's ships.

As the Swordfish droned away from the sinking submarine, the crew sighted the German destroyer *Köllner* slinking into a small fiord to wait in ambush for the British. The observer lost no time in radioing the news back to *Warspite*, and Whitworth ordered the destroyers *Bedouin* and *Eskimo* to make ready for action. When the two ships came to the opening of the *Köllner*'s 'hide' it was with torpedo tubes at the ready and guns trained for action. Far from the *Köllner* surprising the British ships, the position was reversed, and when the German ship came into the British sights, guns opened up and torpedoes slid into the water. Within a few minutes, the *Köllner* was ablaze. But the final *coup de grâce* was dealt by *Warspite*'s heavy guns. The bewildered Germans didn't know what had hit them and their ship sank to the bottom.

On the British force swept until, farther up the fiord, they were met by four German destroyers which opened fire on them. The fire-power of the British force out-matched that of the Germans, and they were forced to turn and flee. But then they soon had their backs to the wall and had to fight. As the big ships of the Royal Navy were about to lash their opponents with fire, Swordfish of the Fleet Air Arm swept in on the German destroyers in a dive-bombing attack. Their strike was wasted, however, since the Germans had room to manoeuvre and evade the falling bombs, and anti-aircraft guns on board the German destroyers claimed two of the British planes.

The Swordfish flew off while the *Warspite* and its attendant destroyers blasted away at the German ships. One of the Germans, the *Künne*, attempted an escape, only to be hunted down by *Eskimo* and destroyed by a furious barrage of fire. But the British ships were not having it all their own way. The *Punjabi* came under heavy fire and sustained several hits which seriously damaged her and caused many casualties. Wounded and unable to continue the battle, she was forced to retreat for a while before gamely coming back for more.

Then the German destroyer, *Giese*, tried to make a break for it and ran straight into a curtain of shell fire from the British ships, which now blocked the harbour entrance. She was dealt with quickly and was soon mortally wounded. Her crew realised this and abandoned ship, leaving her floating aimlessly about the harbour.

Minutes later, the *Cossack* made a dash into the harbour but found herself under attack from the *Roeder* which lay alongside the pier. The *Roeder*'s shells slashed into *Cossack* causing her severe damage, and knocking her steering out of action, which sent her careering across the harbour until she was run aground.

It was then that the *Foxhound* sped into the harbour, hoping to come alongside the *Roeder* which was once more burning furiously. But when the *Foxhound*'s captain noticed German sailors scurrying away from the ship he thought something was wrong, and luckily steered his ship away from the German. Seconds later, the *Roeder* blew up, shattered into a thousand pieces, and all that remained of the German ship was a pall of thick, black smoke.

As for the remaining German ships, their ammunition was fast running out, and they were almost at the mercy of the British warships. But they were still determined to fight to the bitter end, and scurried up a long fiord, the entrance to which lay near Narvik itself. Five of the British destroyers, however, were hot on the enemy's heels, and the chase was on.

Eskimo, in the van of the chase, came face to face with two Germans and they exchanged fire. For a moment the Germans thought they had the advantage, until *Hero* and *Forester* swept up alongside *Eskimo*, and added to the already heavy bombardment of the enemy ships. One of the German destroyers, the *Lüdemann*, scurried off up to the head of the fiord to join the *Arnim* and the *Zenker*, while the remaining destroyer, the *Thiele*, was left to fend for herself against three British ships.

Although the *Thiele* was short on shells, she still had a supply of torpedoes and her captain meant to use them as best he could. He fired a salvo which hit *Eskimo*, blowing her bows clean off and wrecking most of her main armament. In spite of this, one of *Eskimo*'s guns continued firing as if nothing had happened. While *Eskimo* struggled stern-first away from the action, the *Thiele* sped headlong into the shore and scuttled.

By then other British destroyers were dashing up the fiord to come to the aid of *Hero* and *Forester*, but when the combined force of British ships finally reached the head of the fiord they found the German ships run aground and sinking. The German crews could take no more and had decided to leave the fight for another day.

In two determined attacks by British warships, first led by Warburton-Lee and then by Whitworth, the Royal Navy had sunk or completely destroyed ten German destroyers—a handsome reward for two days' work.

For his courage and daring in leading the first attack, Captain Warburton-Lee was posthumously awarded the Victoria Cross—the first to be awarded in the Second World War.

Although the Royal Navy was unable to stop Hitler landing his forces in and occupying Norway, it had dealt the German naval forces a serious blow by destroying ten of her warships and sinking a submarine.

There is a theory put forward by some historians that Hitler was obliged to forget any ideas he had about the invasion of Great Britain, not altogether because of the Royal Air Force's victory in the Battle of Britain, but because the Royal Navy had destroyed so many of his ships that he was incapable of mounting an effective protective naval force for his invading forces. However true that theory might be, one thing is certain, that the Battle of Narvik gave Hitler and his navy chiefs cause for grave concern.

The raid on Narvik, and the ultimate destruction of the German forces there, had another effect, not on the Germans but upon the Norwegians. After the Nazi onslaught, the morale of the people of Norway was naturally at its lowest. But when word spread throughout the country of the Royal Navy's victory at Narvik the people were given new heart, and a ray of hope gleamed for them on a dark horizon. They were shown in one swift action that the Nazi hordes were not super-human and, if the will to fight was there, they could be beaten.

7

Raider at Large

The pursuit and destruction of the 41,700-ton German battleship *Bismarck* in May 1941 will in all probability remain one of the greatest naval encounters of all time. The chase is almost unique in naval history in that it was by the combined efforts of the Royal

Navy, the Fleet Air Arm and the Royal Air Force, that *Bismarck* was finally tracked down. Had it not been for the close co-operation of these three forces, the chase might never have reached a successful conclusion.

The story of *Bismarck*'s epic voyage is one charged with tension, excitement, disaster and courage on both sides. It began in 1936, when work started on building the colossal battleship, one which Adolf Hitler hoped would, along with the others in the German fleet, give Germany mastery of the seas and thus make his quest for the spread of Nazism easier.

Bismarck was eventually launched with great pomp and pageantry in February 1939, only a few months before the outbreak of the Second World War, but a great deal of work had yet to be done on her before she was to be ready for her rôle as a surface raider amid the Atlantic sea lanes.

She was fitted with armour capable of withstanding heavy punishment from enemy guns. Her main armament consisted of eight 15-inch guns and her secondary fire-power of twelve 5·9-inch guns. This vast array of weapons was supplemented by forty anti-aircraft guns and she was designed to have a speed of 31 knots with a range of 8,000 miles.

When the *Bismarck* was nearing completion her gun crews were trained to perfection but it was in May 1941 that she was finally ready to play her part in the war at sea. On the 18th of that month, under the command of Admiral Lütjens, she sailed from Gdynia in the Baltic with her attendant heavy-cruiser *Prinz Eugen*.

Majestically coursing their way through the sea, the two ships passed through the Kattegat and on through the Skagerrak until they reached the North Sea where they steered along the coast of Norway to Korsfiord, near Bergen, and put in to refuel.

Admiral Lütjens was filled with excitement at the thought of the mission that lay ahead of him. His orders were clear. *Bismarck* and *Prinz Eugen* were to break out into the Atlantic and sink as many British merchant ships as possible and remain at battle readiness for as long as they could before finally returning to Germany.

On the same day that they arrived at Korsfiord, an RAF Coastal Command aircraft on a reconnaissance flight sighted the unmistakable shape of *Bismarck* and the smaller *Prinz Eugen* in the fiord and the pilot lost no time in racing back to base to raise the alarm. News of the ships' presence in the fiord was flashed to Admiral Tovey, the Commander-in-Chief Home Fleet, and it did not take the Admiral long to figure out what these two ships were up to. He swung into action immediately.

Tovey signalled HMS *Hood*, the thirty-year-old battle-cruiser, and the heavy-cruiser *Prince of Wales*, ordering them to sail from Scapa Flow to Iceland to help block *Bismarck*'s way into the Atlantic from the North Sea. Meanwhile, the cruisers *Norfolk* and *Suffolk*, the latter of which was fitted with the latest radar system, were patrolling the Denmark Straits, a likely route for *Bismarck* and *Prinz Eugen* to take into the Atlantic. When *Bismarck* and her companion ship made the break the Royal Navy was to be ready.

But that night, just before midnight, the two German ships sailed out of the fiord and set course for the Denmark Straits under cover of darkness through the most appalling weather. The ships pitched and heaved in the angry seas while rain and snow storms lashed their decks. But at last they were under way to do the job they had been built for. Lütjens and *Bismarck*'s captain, Captain Lindemann, were happy. The bad weather at least gave them cover from the prying eyes of reconnaissance aircraft and helped to screen them from any British ships which might be in their area.

The following day, an aircraft of the Fleet Air Arm flew over the Korsfiord and the observer, Commander Rotherham, was aghast when he discovered that the ships had gone in the night. He signalled the news to Admiral Tovey who acted quickly. The raiders were at large and Tovey meant to stop them. He ordered the flagship *King George V*, four cruisers and the aircraft carrier *Victorious* to sail from Scapa Flow immediately. They had not long left Scapa when they were joined by the battle-cruiser *Repulse* and set course for a position south of Iceland.

As the British task force ploughed through the wild seas *Bismarck* and *Prinz Eugen* were sailing towards the Denmark Straits. Speed was imperative for the German ships because not before they were in the open Atlantic would they be able to join up with their support ships, the submariners, oil tankers and scout ships which were lying in wait for them in the ocean.

Eventually the two giants entered the Straits and the following morning dawned thick with fog. The weather was so bad that the British reconnaissance planes which had hoped to scour the seas for *Bismarck* were grounded, and still the German ships felt their way through the dense fog along the edge of the Greenland ice pack. All day they remained undetected until dusk when, onboard the cruiser *Suffolk* a look-out gave a shout. He had spotted two ships emerging from a heavy snow storm about seven miles away from where *Suffolk* was positioned.

Suffolk's crew raced to action stations and the British

ship drew up to full speed then dodged into the fog after locating the enemy ships on her radar. To do battle with the Germans would have been suicidal for *Suffolk* and *Norfolk*, which eventually joined in. Their task was to shadow the big ships until the British battle-cruisers could come into action. As she slipped through the fog and took up position behind the enemy ships, *Suffolk* continued to send out signals telling of their position.

HMS *Hood* and *Prince of Wales* immediately altered course at full speed to intercept *Bismarck* and *Prinz Eugen* fighting their way through the swelling seas to come to grips with the enemy.

At 05·35 hours on the morning of 24 May, look-outs on *Hood* and *Prince of Wales* saw the shapes of the two German ships emerging from a bank of fog. The adversaries had sighted each other and one of the most famous naval battles in history was about to begin.

Hood, at 42,100 tons, was a match for the *Bismarck* in all respects, except that she did not have the German's heavy armour to protect herself. She was capable of equalling *Bismarck*'s 31 knots and her guns, eight 15-inch guns and twelve 5.5-inch guns, matched those of the German battle-cruiser.

The roar of the big guns of *Hood* and *Prince of Wales* were the first to sound in that fearful battle, followed almost immediately by the crash of the German weapons. Admiral Lütjens ordered his gunners to concentrate on *Hood* while Admiral Holland, commander of the British ships, ordered his gunners to fire at the leading German ship, thinking it was *Bismarck*. He was in fact wrong in his belief and his shells arced through the sky towards *Prinz Eugen*.

But Captain Leach of the *Prince of Wales* spotted the mistake and swung his guns on to *Bismarck*. The first of the two British ships to fall victim to the terrifying German fire-power was the *Hood*, straddled by shells from *Prinz Eugen*. One of the shells smashed into the superstructure amidships and started a raging fire but the ships continued to blast away at each other with great clouds of black smoke belching from their gun turrets when they fired shell after shell. The already heaving seas became a boiling cauldron of water as shells plunged into the water hurtling huge columns of sea into the air.

Again and again, *Hood* was hit by the rapid fire of the German ships then a well-aimed salvo hit her amidships again. Seconds later, flames leapt high into the sky out of *Hood*, followed by an ear-splitting explosion. Thick clouds of yellow-white smoke shot upwards from the *Hood* with the fragmented metal rocketing hundreds of feet into the air. For an instant only the bow and stern of the ship could be seen by the horror-struck watchers on board *Prince of Wales*. Then the last remnants of the *Hood* disappeared, leaving only a towering column of smoke. The biggest warship in the British fleet had been literally blown to bits when a shot from *Bismarck* pierced her magazine.

With the *Hood* gone, the concentrated fire-power of both the German ships was turned on *Prince of Wales*. Shells rained out of the sky on to and around the British cruiser until a 15-inch shell smashed into her bridge, killing everybody on it except the captain and a signalman. Two hits below the waterline let tons of water gush into the ship. With half her main armament blasted out of action and taking in sea she had no choice but to make smoke and break off the action. Under cover of her smoke screen *Prince of Wales* escaped the German guns and joined *Suffolk* and *Norfolk* to shadow the enemy vessels.

The valiant fight put up by *Prince of Wales* had not been entirely in vain. She had in fact scored two hits on *Bismarck*, causing an oil leak which forced *Bismarck* to reduce speed to 24 knots, a vital factor in the battles which were to come. A huge oil slick trailing behind *Bismarck* bore witness to the fact that she had been dealt a severe blow.

Lütjens was now in a quandary as to what his course of action should be. With reduced speed, *Bismarck* was no longer the supreme fighting ship she had been and, after a bitter argument between him and Lindemann, he decided to set course for St Nazaire on the coast of German-occupied France where he would make repairs then return to his mission in the Atlantic. But before he did so, *Bismarck* turned on *Suffolk* and fired several salvos. While they were doing battle, *Prinz Eugen* slipped away into the Atlantic, unseen by the British ships.

The loss of the *Hood* had dealt a crushing blow to the British Navy but now the entire fleet was hell-bent on revenge. No matter what the cost, they were determined to send the *Bismarck* to the bottom, for out of *Hood*'s 1,419-man crew only three men survived.

Admiral Tovey, as determined as everyone else in the fleet to sink the *Bismarck*, now brought up his air-craft carrier *Victorious*. She was 100 miles from *Bismarck* when Lieutenant Commander Eugene Esmonde assembled his aircrews and they clambered into the open cockpits of their Swordfish torpedo-bombers on the heaving and pitching deck of *Victorious*. Wind and rain swept the decks as the carrier turned into the wind so that the aircraft could take off.

Esmonde's mission was to locate *Bismarck* and lead the attack with his nine Swordfish to torpedo the floating colossus. In the prevailing weather conditions,

Esmonde's job was to be difficult enough but it was to be made doubly difficult by the type of aircraft he was obliged to use for the attack.

The Swordfish, nicknamed the 'Stringbag' by its aircrews because of its mass of struts and wires, had been declared obsolete even before the war began but without a sufficient number of alternative types of torpedo-bombers, the Fleet Air Arm had to make do with these antiquated biplanes. Powered by a single Pegasus engine, the Swordfish was slow and cumbersome and could muster a top speed of only 135 mph but when it was loaded with its 16,000 pound torpedo, it could barely reach a speed of 85 mph which made it a sitting duck for enemy gunners. Its three-man crew—pilot, observer and air-gunner—were further hampered by the open cockpits which allowed all the weather to soak into them. But in spite of their difficulties men of the Fleet Air Arm performed deeds of unparalleled heroism in these clumsy aircraft.

The deck of *Victorious* shuddered when the nine aircraft engines thundered into life and one by one they took off into the blinding rain and formed up in the grim, black sky. As they forged their way through the driving wind, the rain lashed into their cockpits, soaking the aircrews, getting everywhere—into clothes, into oxygen masks, and adding discomfort to the danger that grew steadily closer.

The Stringbags clawed their way through the weather until a tell-tale blip appeared on their airborne radar sets. It was almost midnight and conditions couldn't have been worse for their attack on *Bismarck*.

Suddenly, through the darkness they sighted the German ship pounding though the waves. Esmonde rattled off his battle orders and the squadron broke up to launch a three-pronged attack on the ship.

One by one their noses dipped towards the sea and they thundered on *Bismarck*. Tracer bullets laced through the sky smashing into the the canvas-covered aircraft but still the Stringbags droned on through the unrelenting wall of fire and flak until, half a mile from the *Bismarck*, they released their 'tin fish'. The torpedoes plunged into the water and sped towards the ship, leaving a phosphorescent trail of bubbles behind them. Alas only one of the torpedoes hit the ship, scoring a blow amidships, but the resulting explosion did little damage and failed to penetrate the 15-inch armour plating on the giant's hull.

Bitterly disappointed, Esmonde led his aircraft off into the black night and fierce storm and back to the heaving deck of *Victorious*. The air attack had failed to inflict a mortal wound on *Bismarck* but the determined and courageous attack by the Fleet Air Arm left Lütjens in no doubt about the resolution of the Royal Navy to attack his ship with every possible means at their disposal.

Bismarck steamed on through a fierce Atlantic swell. With reduced speed and the thought that as many British ships as could be mustered were speeding to do battle with him, Lütjens realised that his only chance of survival lay in giving his hunters the slip.

On the morning of the 25th, the pursuers expected to close up on *Bismarck* and join once more in battle but when dawn came and anxious look-outs surveyed the horizon the German ship was nowhere to be seen. Lütjens had succeeded in giving them the slip. A frantic search got under way.

Later, on board *Bismarck*, Lütjens was itching to tell the German people at home of his spectacular victory over the *Hood* and he signalled a lengthy message to Germany, thinking that he was still within the radar net of the British ships and could do no harm by making the signal. Had he but known it, the British ships had lost contact with him six hours before but when his message was flashed to Germany, it was intercepted and the plotters got to work getting a fix on the *Bismarck*. As bad luck would have it, a miscalculation put *Bismarck* on a course north-east towards the Iceland-Faroes passage. When Tovey received the news he immediately directed his ships, many of them short on fuel, north, in a bid to block *Bismarck*'s way into the North Sea. But in the meantime *Bismarck* was sailing south.

Through the night and into the morning of the 26th the British ships searched but there was no sign of *Bismarck*. She had well and truly slipped through the net and had it not been for the RAF's Coastal Command, *Bismarck* might have reached St Nazaire without interception.

At 10.30 hours on that morning, fateful as it was to be for the *Bismarck*, an RAF Catalina flying-boat droned over the rolling Atlantic waves and the crew caught sight of the lone ship, its bows dipping and rising in the swell. There was no mistaking it—they had found *Bismarck*. At last the British knew where she was but, by then, Tovey and his warships were too far away to give effective chase and had little hope of closing up with the enemy. Through lack of fuel many of the hunters had to return to Britain. But the Navy still had one ace up its sleeve. A force of British ships, under the command of Admiral Somerville, was steaming at top speed from the Mediterranean to intercept *Bismarck*. More important, Somerville had with him the aircraft-carrier *Ark Royal* which carried more Swordfish aircraft.

It was vital, if the British ships were to deliver the

fatal blow to *Bismarck*, to slow her down and with this in mind, another Swordfish attack was planned. With the carrier's flight deck pitching in the violent seas in a 56 foot arc, fifteen Swordfish took off but one soon had to turn back leaving fourteen to battle against the howling wind and reach the target.

As the fourteen Swordfish fought through the blinding rain and low cloud, the cruiser *Sheffield* took up a position astern of the *Bismarck* and began tracking her with radar. At last the German raider was caught in an invisible electronic beam and there was to be no escaping for her now.

In the Swordfish, the crews cursed the weather. It could not have been worse for the attack. Visibility was dangerously poor but nevertheless they were determined to fight on and deliver their torpedoes.

Observers gazed intently at their radar, waiting for the tell-tale blip on their screens which would pinpoint the target. Then it was there. Courses were altered to bring them on to their target and they dived down to attack height. The pilots strained their eyes to catch sight of the enemy ship, then a blurred shape appeared through the driving rain. With throttles wide open the Swordfish thundered into the attack.

Meanwhile on board the cruiser *Sheffield*, look-outs spotted the Swordfish charging in towards *their* ship. Some gave a yell as they recognised the friendly aircraft and acknowledged their comrades with a wave. Then the cheery waves turned to gasps of horror as they realised the awful truth . . .

'Stone the crows!' a look-out screamed. 'They're attacking!'

Eleven of the Swordfish soared in, launching their 'fish' at the *Sheffield*. In the blinding rain the pilots had mistaken it for *Bismarck*. Now the *Sheffield* dodged around in the waves trying desperately to avoid the lethal sausage-shaped torpedoes as they sliced through the water towards her. Luckily, five of the torpedoes detonated prematurely, three of the pilots recognised their mistake and broke off their attacks in time, and *Sheffield*'s captain managed to dodge the remainder. The pilots had thought it strange that they were not met by a barrage of fire when they attacked the ship.

The mistake could have ended in disaster but luckily it did not, and the Swordfish made their way back to the *Ark Royal* and landed on her pitching deck. The near calamity had provided them with some valuable truths. There was a serious defect in their torpedoes and the magnetic detonators were removed and replaced with impact detonators.

The aircrews who had mistakenly attacked *Sheffield* were now even more determined to put paid to the *Bismarck* and with their Swordfish refuelled and loaded with torpedoes, they took off again into the raging storm. This time there would be no mistaking the enemy and the Swordfish battled through the elements until at last they found *Bismarck*. But *Bismarck*'s gun crews were instantly at battle stations and pumping shells and bullets into the air, facing the attackers with a furious barrage.

One by one the Swordfish charged in to attack, with shell splinters and bullets ripping through their flimsy fuselages while *Bismarck* zig-zagged in the mountainous Atlantic waves. The first eleven torpedoes launched failed to hit the target and two other aircraft could not launch their 'tin fish' because they had jammed. There were now only two torpedoes left and if the raid was to be success, these two 'fish' had to find their mark.

The fourteenth Swordfish droned in towards *Bismarck* and dropped its torpedo before banking violently to escape the anti-aircraft fire. The 'fish' coursed through the water and hit *Bismarck* amidships without effect. That left only one aircraft to deliver the final fatal blow.

Hope faded that *Bismarck* would be damaged at all but the last Swordfish soared in for its attack. At the last moment, her torpedo crashed into the water and raced for *Bismarck*. It ran true and hit the *Bismarck*'s hull, exploding and wrecking the ship's steering engine room.

From the air, there seemed to be no visible damage and the pilots and crews of the Swordfish thought that their raid had been a complete failure. But they had in fact inflicted a mortal wound on the pride of the German navy. The torpedo had struck while *Bismarck*'s rudder was hard over and nothing that the German crew could do would unstick it. *Bismarck* could do nothing but sail in circles. Her end was close at hand.

With *Sheffield* now bearing down on her, *Bismarck* showed that she still had teeth and fired a broadside which sent the smaller British ship scurrying out of range under cover of smoke. *Bismarck*'s shells had killed three of *Sheffield*'s crew and smashed her radar. But *Sheffield* signalled home that the *Bismarck* was steering a crazy course and actually heading *towards* her hunters.

On board the stricken German ship, divers worked frantically in the flooded engine room to repair the damage but their attempts were in vain. Admiral Lütjens realised only too well that *Bismarck* was in her death throes—but he was not going to give up without a fight.

Throughout the night *Bismarck* was attacked continuously by torpedoes from the 4th Destroyer flotilla, under the command of Captain Vian, which formed a ring around the German. The destroyers swept in and fired their torpedoes, then dashed out of range, but alas, none of the torpedoes scored a hit.

With the coming of dawn. Vian called off his attack. Although he had not caused *Bismarck* any damage, he knew that her gunners must be physically exhausted, having fought continuously throughout the night. Now it was the turn of the British capital ships to come into the battle.

At 08.47 hours, *King George V* and *Rodney* closed in for the attack with their 14- and 15-inch guns pounding away at *Bismarck*. Desperately, the German ship replied but to no avail. Shells smashed into the German ship, tearing its superstructure apart, wiping out the bridge, gun turrets, demolishing her funnel and felling her towering masts. A raging inferno swept throughout the ship as more shells rained down on her with murderous effect—and yet the pride of the German navy remained afloat taking this terrible punishment.

The British battleships closed in and brought their secondary armament to bear on the flaming colossus, and the heavy cruiser, *Norfolk*, hero of the earlier battle with *Bismarck*, closed in to fire torpedoes which missed. By then, the battleships were a mere two miles away from *Bismarck*, almost point-blank range in a sea battle, and they were pumping continuous salvos of shells into her. Finally, short of fuel, the two battleships called off their attack, but not before *Rodney* had fired a torpedo and scored a hit on *Bismarck*.

Norfolk soared in and unleashed a further four torpedoes but still the German remained afloat. Amazingly, her engines were still working perfectly, the heavy armour plating on her sides having protected them. But with her top side a mass of tangled steel and blazing furiously, she could not survive for very much longer, and it was to be left to the heavy cruiser

Dorsetshire to deal the final blow. She fired two torpedoes at the blazing hulk, one of which scored a hit and exploded. The German giant could take it no longer.

At 10.40 hours the *Bismarck* capsized to port amid a boiling cauldron of water, and with her flag still flying she sank into the depths. The German giant, which Hitler had thought would sever Britain's trans-Atlantic lifeline, had been at large for less than six whole days and not one single merchantman had fallen to her guns. The sinking of *Hood* had been avenged.

8

Raid on St Nazaire

A deep-throated deafening roar echoed over Falmouth harbour as the engines of sixteen Royal Navy motor launches burst into life at 14.00 hours on the afternoon of 26 March 1942. The fanfare of noise heralded the beginning of one of the most daring raids in naval history—the attack on St Nazaire.

The port of St Nazaire, situated at the mouth of the River Loire on the Atlantic coast of German-occupied France, housed the only dry dock big enough to take the 45,500-ton German battle-cruiser *Tirpitz*. At that time the *Tirpitz*, sister ship to the ill-fated *Bismarck*, lay bottled up in a Norwegian fiord, waiting for her chance to slip into the North Sea and then the Atlantic. Once at large in the Atlantic, *Tirpitz* could play havoc with the Allied convoys bringing war supplies and food to Britain from the United States and Canada. Britain's Prime Minister, Winston Churchill, was only too aware of the enormous threat that *Tirpitz* posed and the potential disaster she could cause and he ordered that she be destroyed at all costs.

The German High Command realised what a powerful weapon they had at their command and knew full well that once in the Atlantic, *Tirpitz* could play a vital part in turning the tide of the war in favour of the Germans by 'strangling' the British Isles and denying her the precious supplies that enabled her to continue the conflict with Germany.

But the Germans also knew that no warship of that size could operate successfully for any length of time without a safe dry-dock to return to for maintenance and repair and the only one big enough in the Atlantic was the Normandie dock at St Nazaire.

This dock was the biggest of its kind in the world and had been specially built to accommodate the French ocean liner *Normandie*. It formed a huge pool, 1,148 feet in length and 164 feet wide, and at either end of it were two great movable lock-gates, known as caissons. Because of their size, these lock-gates were unlike anything that had ever been constructed before. Each one of these caissons slid on rollers and were vast constructions measuring 167 feet in length, 54 feet in height and 35 feet in thickness. They were built of steel and comprised of a series of water-tight compartments which could be filled with water when required to withstand the varying pressures involved in filling and emptying the dock.

It was obvious that moving these vast gates required enormous power and each of them had a power-house and winding mechanism by its side as well as a pump-house in which were housed the huge pumps used to empty the dock of water.

In the Nazaire basin, not far from the Normandie dock, was a cluster of bomb-proof submarine pens which acted as a refuge for the 'wolf packs' of German U-boats which scoured the Atlantic, preying on Allied shipping.

The Germans, knowing how vital the dock area was to them in their war in the Atlantic, took no chances. The whole shore-line bristled with searchlights and guns, ranging in size from 20 to 40 mm. To give the base further security from a sea-borne attack there was a natural hazard any attacking force would have to face—the extensive mud flats and shoal water. Only one deep path, known as the Charpentiers Channel, existed which could take ships big enough to mount a worthwhile attack on St Nazaire and that was 'covered' from the banks of the river by a concentration of guns. St Nazaire was impregnable—or so the Germans thought.

Among the British armed forces there was an organisation known as Combined Operations which was commanded by Admiral Lord Louis Mountbatten, a resourceful and courageous sailor with a distinguished naval career behind him. The purpose of Combined Operations was to pool the resources of the three armed services for special raids, designed to hit the enemy where they least expected it and to execute clandestine attacks on vital objectives which would make it more difficult for the Axis forces to carry on the war.

Manpower and material could be drawn from all three services for these raids, but to be of maximum use to the war effort Mountbatten and his staff had to choose their targets carefully. They pondered for hours over maps, sifted through every piece of information that came out of occupied territory and examined thousands of photographs of enemy-occupied Europe taken by RAF reconnaissance aircraft. Nothing was allowed to escape their attention lest it should spark off an idea which could lead to a raid and at all times they had to have a complete picture of the progress of the war in every sector of operations. It was not long, therefore, before the port of St Nazaire came to their attention and the possibility of putting it out of action was investigated.

On first examination, a raid on St Nazaire seemed almost impossible. That is, until Mountbatten mobilised his staff. Not only did they produce detailed maps of the Loire estuary and aerial reconnaissance photographs of the docks but, most amazingly of all, a detailed drawing of the dock layout with highly accurate drawings of the caissons and how they were constructed. In fact the information was so detailed that they were able to build a scale model of the exact layout of the entire dock area showing the dock, submarine pens, buildings, searchlight positions and gun positions exactly as they were in reality.

But having all that information, vital as it was, was not enough. They had to discover some way of penetrating the defences and destroying the Normandie dock. Attack from the air by RAF Bomber Command was out, as there was at that time no bomb powerful enough to inflict permanent damage on the huge lock-gates. The only alternative seemed to be a sea-borne attack but, as has been seen, this seemed to mean an operation of almost suicidal proportions because of the concentrated defences covering the Charpentiers Channel.

It was obvious that, to stand any chance at all of

reaching the target, an attacking force would have to sail across the mud flats. But any ship big enough to carry the number of men it would require for demolition work, both on the dock gates and subsidiary targets, would get stuck in the mud banks. The staff of Combined Operations racked their brains for a solution until Captain Hughes-Hallett RN came up with a brilliant solution. Why not, he suggested, use a destroyer as the weapon of attack? Pack explosives into the hull of the ship and ram the lock-gate, then when the destroyer was stuck fast, a pre-set delayed-action time device would enable the crew to get off before the whole thing blew up, destroying the huge caissons. Support forces in the form of commandos who would give cover fire and carry out additional demolition work on the caissons, winding house and pump house along with the subsidiary targets, could be carried to the scene of the attack on board a fleet of Royal Navy motor launches.

Hughes-Hallett's plan was indeed a daring one and Mountbatten and his group of planners studied it closely. It might just work, they decided, and day and night they studied every tiny detail. It was agreed that the attack would have to take place at night and Bomber Command would carry out a raid on St Nazaire just as the attacking naval force was approaching in the hope that the German defenders would be too pre-occupied with the air-raid to notice the attackers coming in from the sea. Every possible eventuality was considered and by the end of February the plan was approved. But they had to act quickly. In order to give the raiders plenty of time to carry out their attack under cover of darkness, the attack would have to take place before the end of March as the nights were becoming shorter. Furthermore, experts figured that towards the end of March the state of the tides would be such that there would be enough water in the Loire estuary to allow the destroyer to sail over the mud flats without becoming stuck fast. Mountbatten had only one month in which to get the raid organised, men trained and ships assembled for the operation.

Two men were appointed to lead the attack, Lieutenant-Colonel A. C. Newman and Commander R. E. D. Ryder RN. Newman would lead the commandos and Ryder the naval attacking force. Both men were hand picked and eminently qualified for the job.

Newman was in command of No 2 Commando and he set about training his men to the peak of physical fitness. They practised landings, scaling cliffs and street fighting. They went on marathon route marches, sleeping rough and toughening themselves up to hard fighting men. Newman realising that many of his men had never been to sea before insisted that they 'got their sea legs'. He knew they would have to endure a long sea journey before the raid and he did not wish to arrive at St Nazaire with shiploads of sea-sick soldiers. So he sent them to sea with the Royal Navy in all weathers.

While Newman continued to train his men and teach them all there was to know about the use of explosives, Ryder was equally hard at work organising the naval force. He gathered together his fleet of motor launches which had to be specially converted for the raid. Additional fuel tanks were fitted for the long voyage and their existing 3-pounder guns replaced by Oerlikon 20 mm. heavy machine-guns. These sleek 112 foot long 'B' Class launches were powered by 650 hp petrol engines and were capable of speeds up to eighteen knots and the addition of the two 500-

gallon fuel tanks increased their range from 600 to about 1,000 miles.

The biggest problem of all, however, was finding a suitable destroyer, which was both expendable and available for the task. Ryder hunted high and low until he discovered HMS *Campbeltown*. This ship was one of fifty obsolete destroyers leased to Britain by the United States at the outbreak of the war. *Campbeltown* was ideally suited for the job but for the attack certain modifications were essential and work began immediately when she arrived at Devonport.

It was vital to reduce the draught of *Campbeltown* so that she would not run aground on the mud flats in the Loire estuary so workmen busied themselves removing the main armament of three four-inch guns, the torpedo tubes, depth charges and their throwers. Two of the four funnels were removed and the remaining two were 'raked off' to make them resemble the conventional German funnels. It was hoped that by doing this, *Campbeltown* might be mistaken for a German warship by the Nazaire defenders.

Eight Oerlikon guns were fitted and quarter-inch-thick armour plating fitted around the bridge and the deck to help protect the crew and the commandos *Campbeltown* would carry, from the fire-power of the German guns. But perhaps the most difficult problem with the *Campbeltown* lay in how she would carry the explosives. Many lives would be lost amongst the crew and the commandos if the explosives blew up when *Campbeltown* hit the caissons and the whole show would be a complete waste of time if the Germans discovered the explosives and succeeded in defusing them before they blew up. What, then, were they to do?

Two explosives experts, Lieutenant Nigel Tibbits

of the Royal Navy and Captain Pritchard of the Royal Engineers, were called in to help. Between them they decided that the safest place for the explosives would be just behind the steel pillar which supported the forward gun turret. They calculated that when *Campbeltown* rammed the caissons, the bows would be smashed back as far as the pillar but no further, with the pillar protecting the charge. The explosive charge itself would be comprised of 24 depth-charges encased in a steel tank which would then be enveloped in concrete. Pencil fuses were to be used to denonate the four and a quarter tons of explosives giving a delay of several hours before the blast.

The days passed all too quickly and the pre-raid activity reached fever pitch. Ryder decided that two more boats should be added to the fleet, one motor-torpedo-boat and a motor-gun-boat to give added protection to the attackers.

Newman and Ryder were to go into battle aboard the MGB along with the fleet navigator and a signalman, Leading Signalman Pike, a man who was destined to play an important part in the raid because of his ability to make signals in German. The boat itself fairly bristled with armament, which was just as well, for it was to carry the men who would mastermind the attack. To protect her precious passengers she carried a 2-pounder Vickers pom-pom forward, a two-pounder aft and two twin half-inch heavy machine-guns amidships.

The other newcomer to the fleet was MTB 74, a motor-torpedo-boat with torpedo tubes mounted on the fo'c'sle. This rather unconventional craft was to carry delayed-action torpedoes which were intended to be used against the caissons should *Campbeltown* fail to ram it. But MTB 74 was dogged with engine trouble, and remarkably, was incapable of maintaining a reasonable cruising speed. She could travel at six knots or dash at forty but was unable to maintain any speed in between. The result was that in order to stay with the convoy she would have to be towed most of the way.

Two escorting destroyers were also added to the fleet of ships. They were HMS *Arthurstone* and HMS *Tynedale*; bringing the total number of ships in the force to twenty-one. The naval fleet was now complete and while the final preparations continued, the commandos were hard at work perfecting their part in the attack.

It was discovered that the King George V dock at Southampton was almost identical to the Normandie and night after night the commando demolition teams practised their attack on the dock. By night they climbed into the caissons and planted dummy explosives, just as they planned to do during the real attack and by day they repeated their 'dummy runs'—blindfold. When the time came, they were to know every inch of their target.

Meanwhile other commando parties 'blew up' installations in other dockyards with plastic explosives. They were taught all there was to know about dock-yard machinery and soon learned which ones to blow-up to cause the maximun amount of damage. They studied the model of the dock area layout until it was imprinted in their minds and they knew every single building in it, what it housed and where it was.

Although the commandos realised they were soon to take part in something big, none of them was told where the target was because one slip of the tongue, one careless word could spell disaster for the raiders.

Ryder was a man almost obsessed with the need for security, so much so that he would not even allow Newman or any of his commandos onboard his ships in uniform lest a German spy should put two and two together and realise that a Combined Operations' raid was imminent. Ryder's fears of a 'leak' were perfectly justified for it was known that German spies had infiltrated into most of the major dockyards in Britain.

Such was Newman's attention to detail that before the raid the commandos were issued with special rubber-soled boots and told that, once in St Nazaire, if they heard someone approaching in the darkness whose boots made a crunching noise they were to shoot to kill—he'd be a German! To make doubly sure of friend or foe they were issued with a password, 'War Weapons Week' the reply to which was 'Weymouth'. It was a crafty piece of concoction on Newman's part because he knew perfectly well that the Germans pronounced the letter 'W' as 'V' and would be instantly recognisable as the enemy should the password fall into their hands.

Five days before the raid they carried out a full-scale mock raid on the dockyard at Devonport. From the attackers' point of view the 'raid' was a disaster. They were quickly repelled by units of the Home Guard amongst other dock defenders. But the raid was far from being a waste of time. They learned some valuable lessons that were to stand them in good stead during the real raid.

Then, just 24 hours before the attack was due to begin Colonel Newman revealed the long-awaited secret. The target was to be St Nazaire. The days of uncertainty were over and it was with a sense of relief that the commandos received the news. At least now they knew where their battle-ground was to be.

But late on that same day news reached them that almost put an end to the planned attack. An RAF photo-reconnaissance aircraft brought back pictures of St Nazaire which showed clearly that five *Mowe* class German destroyers were anchored in the St Nazaire basin. Their presence posed a great threat to the success of the mission but with typical dogged determination Colonel Newman refused to be deterred. The raid would go ahead as planned.

That night, the commandos boarded their ships and waited. At 12.30 hours on 26 March a signal came to the waiting force from Admiral Farber. It read, 'Carry out Chariot.' The raid was on.

The armada of ships slipped out of Falmouth followed by *Campbeltown* and the escorting destroyers and set course for the Bay of Biscay. As the fleet rode through the waves at a steady 13 knots, the 265 commandos relaxed as best they could joking amongst each other, playing nonsensical games in a bid to cover the nervousness each of them felt. All of them knew that the conflict that lay ahead would take its inevitable toll of their number but none of them would admit it openly to another or admit that it might be he who would fall to a German bullet. Everything that was humanly possible by way of precise and accurate planning and training had been done but the greatest danger of all lay in the unexpected. No one knew how the Germans would react to the raid. They could only resign themselves to waiting.

Resolutely the ships sailed on into the evening until darkness closed in while the commandos and the crew not on watch settled down to an uneasy sleep. The night passed without incident but that happy state of affairs was not to last. By dawn they had reached a point south of St Nazaire. It was then that trouble began. A look-out aboard the escort destroyer *Tynedale* sighted a ship on the horizon and crews raced to action stations. On the bridge of the destroyer, the captain scanned the horizon through powerful binoculars. It was a U-boat. He ordered a change of course at full speed ahead. *Tynedale* swept round and sped off towards the submarine leaving a bubbling, foaming wake behind her. The U-boat crew did not notice the oncoming destroyer until *Tynedale* was within a mile of her. Then the Klaxon blared and the German crew dashed off the deck and tumbled down the conning tower.

Tynedale's guns burst into life with a thundering roar but the U-boat was already plunging beneath the surface amid a boiling sea of foam. As the submarine disappeared from sight into the sanctuary of the ocean's depths, *Tynedale*'s shells exploded shooting great plumes of white sea into the air.

When *Tynedale* reached the U-boat's position she unleashed a pattern of depth charges which sent sea heaving and bursting skywards with the violent explosions. Then to the amazement of the British captain and crew, the U-boat surfaced once more, only to be hit by a fusillade of shells from *Tynedale* before diving one more and disappearing to lie on the ocean bed.

No one could be sure about whether or not *Tynedale* had destroyed the submarine and repeated sweeps of the area revealed nothing. Two hours later the search was abandoned and the destroyers steamed off out into the Atlantic in the hope that if they were spotted it would be assumed that they were part of an anti-submarine operation. It was as well that they did, for when the German submarine surfaced, it reported sighting Ryder's fleet of ships and the German naval command ordered the five *Mowe* class destroyers out of St Nazaire into the Atlantic to search for them. That, at least, removed one formidable obstacle which had lain in the path of Ryder's ships and they got underway once more. But it was not long before they were in action again.

Shortly after their encounter with the U-boat, a fleet of French fishing vessels was sighted and this gave Ryder cause for some concern. He knew that some French trawlers carried German naval observers with radio equipment and he could not take a chance on the Germans being forewarned of the impending attack. He had no alternative but to order the French crews off the boats, take them on board then sink their trawlers. A third trawler was boarded by sailors, the crew taken off then it too was shelled. The captain of one of the ill-fated trawlers assured Ryder that there were no German observers onboard any of the other trawlers still afloat and Ryder left them to their fishing and set off once more.

The day passed into evening as the fleet made its somewhat erratic deception course towards its target and tension mounted to a peak when they arrived at a point where Newman and Ryder changed ships and went aboard the MGB, the craft from which they were to lead the attack. They pressed on into the night and at 22.15 hours, precisely on time, spotted the welcome flash signals from the British submarine *Sturgeon*. She had been lurking there waiting to point the way into the Loire to the fleet of ships.

On the ships went into the estuary but no sooner had they done so when *Campbeltown* ground to a halt with a sickening shudder. She was aground on a mud shoal. Instantly the prospect of remaining in this highly vulnerable position shot through the minds of crew and commandos alike. Aground, high and dry she would be a sitting duck. But luckily she succeeded in struggling off the shoal—only to run aground again a few minutes later. It was with an enormous sigh of relief that she eventually managed to drive out of the mud and continue on her course once more.

Now that she was free of the treacherous mud, the fuses on the explosives stowed in *Campbeltown* were set to detonate eight hours later. There was no turning back now. The point of no return had been reached and nothing could stop the explosives from blowing up now. All that remained was to guide *Campbeltown* to St Nazaire and ram the caissons. But that was to be even more difficult than they had imagined.

The bewitching hour of midnight drew closer and as it did so, the drone of heavy aircraft engines reached the ears of the defenders in St Nazaire. Pencil-thin fingers of light searched the sky as the German searchlights came into action for the raiders. Anti-aircraft guns opened up spreading a barrage of fragmented metal about the sky, while the unmistakable crump of exploding bombs punctuated the din.

The RAF pilots were under orders to drop only one bomb on each run-in on the target area, but this in itself gave rise to suspicion amongst the Germans who were used to more intensive bombing. It soon became obvious that the raid was intended merely as diversion for something bigger and the Germans looked to the sea.

The element of surprise that Ryder had so carefully planned for was immediately lost and the alarm raised. *Campbeltown* had only two more miles to go before impact when suddenly the Loire was a blaze of light as searchlights along the bank swept the river. Instantly *Campbeltown* was bathed in light looking like a great, white ghost ship. The German gunners held their fire, their fingers poised over the triggers of their guns. They did not know what to make of it. The *Campbeltown* certainly looked like a German warship and she was flying the German naval flag but no such convoy of ships was expected. The uneasy seconds ticked by. Someone had to make a move and the Germans were first to take the initiative when signal lights flashed from two stations on the shore.

Leading Signalman Pike, on board Ryder's MGB, waited tensely to play his part in the game of bluff. He raised his signal lamp and flashed the morse code name of one of the German torpedo boats he knew operated in the area. Then he turned his attentions to the other station and signalled that they were a German naval force sailing under orders to anchor in harbour. Amazingly the deception worked and the searchlights went out. Then one of the shore batteries opened fire. Pike immediately signalled that they were being attacked by friendly forces and the firing ceased. But their luck had already been strained to the limits. In an instant every gun on shore opened fire on the fleet. Bullets and shells ripped and tore into the *Campbeltown* gashing the armour plating and taking their toll of the crew. Lieutenant Commander Beattie, captain of the *Campbeltown*, ordered that the German flag be taken down and the white ensign raised. The sight of the British flag fluttering at the masthead enraged the German gunners whose furious barrage of fire grew in intensity. But still the *Campbeltown* ploughed stubbornly on through the whistling shells and tracer bullets.

On board every ship in the fleet guns roared and chattered back in a deafening reply to the German fire and searchlights were pinched out like candles as British guns found their marks.

To Newman and Ryder in the MGB, which was leading the *Campbeltown* to its target, the battle seemed to rage for an eternity while Leading Seaman William Savage, manning the pom-pom, blasted away at everything that moved onshore. The slightest shadow caught the full fury of his fire.

Then the dock gate came into sight and Beattie increased *Campbeltown*'s speed to 20 knots, the speed at which it would ram the caissons. On board the MGB, Lieutenant Curtis, the captain, waited until his boat was dwarfed by the towering gate before he swung her away to starboard giving *Campbeltown* a clear run in to ram.

Campbeltown's engines were going full blast as she shook and shuddered, coursing through the water. From the bridge Beattie ordered a last change of course as the caissons drew nearer. With only a few yards to go, an incendiary bomb hit the fo'c'sle of the ship and burst into flames, engulfing the forward deck of the ship with a raging inferno. But Beattie was not to be swayed from his target.

'Stand by to ram!' he yelled and everyone on board braced themselves for impact. Seconds later it came . . .

A grinding, ear-splitting thunder reverberated through the ship as she shuddered to a halt, crunching and crumpling into the caissons. The colossal bows of the *Campbeltown* were driven back 36 feet under the impact and she mounted the top of the caissons and finally came to a halt. The commandos waiting on her deck leapt off the ship and dashed along the dockside to set about the night's work of destruction.

Meanwhile, the motor launches dashed in towards the shore to unload their parties of commandos and it was then that some of the most disastrous events of the raid took place. As the MLs nosed into their appointed positions to disgorge their loads of commandos, they were met by the full force of the German fire-power.

Caught in the searchlights, the MLs were easy targets for the rapid fire guns the Germans had placed at strategic points along the dock. They poured lead into the wood-built ships and tossed grenades into the boats from the quayside above, shattering the hulls and killing the commandos and crew who were on deck waiting their turn to land. Ships blazed as petrol tanks burst into fire and men leapt in the river only to be swamped in flames by burning petrol on the surface.

Six of the motor launches came under such heavy fire that they were soon just floating furnaces. Other boats were forced to withdraw, unable to penetrate the wall of white-hot metal put up by the German guns. One boat, blazing from stem to stern, drifted out of control towards where the *Campbeltown* was lodged in the caissons. Then it blew up, disintegrating into a thousand pieces.

The scene on the river was one of complete chaos. The mangled wrecks of motor launches were strewn across the river and bathed in light from the powerful searchlights. All this was against a back-cloth of night sky scarred by the rakish lines of multi-coloured tracer trails. The ear-torturing din of battle grew in an almost unbearable crescendo of sound as the chatter of machine-guns and the roar of heavy guns became more and more intense.

Of the entire force of motor launches that succeeded in reaching St Nazaire, only four landed their commandos. One other ML got through only to land a single man.

After landing his party of commandos, Lieutenant Rodier, commanding one of the motor launches, made for the *Campbeltown* and drew alongside it to take onboard Lieutenant Commander Beattie and half of the crew. But they immediately came under heavy fire from German guns. As the boat pulled away from the *Campbeltown*, it was coned in searchlight beams and every gun that could get its range was pumping lead into it. The crew of the *Campbeltown*, huddled on deck, were mown down by the concentrated fire. Beattie, who was on the bridge with Rodier, left it to go and inspect the damage to the rest of the ship and in particular to the engine room which had been badly hit. He had no sooner left the bridge when it received a direct hit by a shell and Rodier was killed. Hungry flames swept through the boat taking a further toll of the men until it finally had to be abandoned. Beattie was one of the handful of men who survived the raging torrent of fire only to spend the rest of the war in captivity.

By then Colonel Newman and Commander Ryder's MGB had reached its off-loading point near the *Campbeltown* and Newman and his headquarters' staff disembarked. As soon as that was done, the remainder of the crew from the *Campbeltown* crowded onboard but Ryder was by no means finished. He wanted to check for himself that everything was set for the big blast onboard the *Campbeltown* so he left the MGB and took a look for himself. He scrambled up on to the *Campbeltown*'s deck and had only taken a few steps when scuttling charges exploded, rocking the ship and sinking it at the stern. This was all part of the plan to make the ship more securely lodged at the caissons and, satisfied that all was prepared satisfactorily, Ryder returned to the MGB.

It was then that Lieutenant Wynn's motor torpedo boat arrived alongside the MGB and Ryder ordered him to fire his delayed action torpedoes at the caisson.

Wasting no time, Wynn manoeuvred the boat into position and with a hiss, the two torpedoes shot out of their tubes on the fo'c'sle and hit the caissons with a resounding thud before sinking to the sea-bed to await detonation.

With his part of the raid completed, Wynn took on-board some more of the *Campbeltown*'s crew from Ryder's MGB then headed for home at full speed. His boat shot past the German guns and none of them could find their mark on the boat which was racing along at forty knots. Then Wynn spotted two men in the water and, typical of the man, he stopped to pick them up. The result was fatal. This was all the German gunners had needed and they drew a bead on the boat and plastered it with bullets and shells. Wynn was one of the first to be seriously wounded. Then the boat caught fire and they were forced to abandon ship and take to a raft. Of the thirty-odd men on that raft, only Wynn and two others survived to be taken prisoner by a German patrol boat after they had drifted out to sea.

Another of the epic escape bids was enacted on board Lieutenant Henderson's motor launch. His boat was one of those which had been forced to withdraw because of the weight of the German defence and had been unable to land its quota of commandos. Henderson set out to sea to rendezvous with waiting British destroyers which were to escort the raiders home but instead of meeting the British destroyers, he ran slap into the five German destroyers which had been in St Nazaire earlier.

It was pitch dark when they caught sight of the German ships dashing through the night towards St Nazaire in answer to a frantic call for help from the dock's defenders. The destroyers were closing in fast but, Henderson hoped, they might not see the motor launch in the darkness so he cut engines and decided to sit it out with fingers crossed. He called for absolute silence onboard as the first of the destroyers slipped past their boat in the gloom. Then came the second and their luck held. The third, the destroyer *Jaguar*, ploughed towards them and their luck was shattered. Suddenly a searchlight from the German ship pierced the darkness and ringed the ML with light but it was almost instantly shattered by a well-aimed burst of fire from the ML. Another searchlight lit up the scene and a battle royal began with a vengeance. Every gun on the ML opened up at the destroyer as well as the commandos' pistols while the German boat poured all it had into the ML. On the bridge of the German destroyer, Lieutenant Paul, the ship's captain, could not believe that the little boat could put up such a furious barrage of fire and he ordered the helmsman to ram the British boat. *Jaguar* swung round in an arc and pounded down on the ML but by then Henderson was wise to Paul's intentions and at the very last moment swung out of the way of the approaching destroyer and took only a glancing blow from its mighty bows.

By then the deck of the ML was strewn with dead and dying men and Lieutenant Paul, in a bid to bring the battle to an end, opened up at the tiny boat with his 4.1-inch gun which gouged great chunks out of the boat and killed Henderson. But those who could muster the strength to do so were determined to continue the fight to its bitter end, no matter what the cost. One of them was Sergeant Durrant, a commando who, already wounded, was to epitomise the courage shown by sailor and soldier alike that night.

Durrant blazed away at the destroyer with his bren

gun, raking it with fire and, when the sailor manning the ML's twin Lewis gun was killed, it was Durrant who hauled himself up to man the gun and pump more bullets at the *Jaguar*. The battle raged on until Lieutenant Paul called to the ML to surrender. But the British weren't having it: Durrant, wounded in at least a dozen places by then, levelled the Lewis gun and blazed away yet again at the destroyer's bridge only narrowly missing the German captain. Seconds later Durrant was hit again and collapsed dying on the deck.

The fight could go on no longer and after a battle that will remain an epic in the history of the Royal Navy's little ships, the remaining Britons reluctantly surrendered to a German crew who were filled with admiration for the courageous fight they had put up against such overwhelming odds.

But meanwhile the battle back at St Nazaire raged furiously amid the crowded dockyard buildings. Colonel Newman witnessed the noise of exploding charges as the work of the demolition squads bore fruit and with their work done they re-assembled for the withdrawal point only to find that the motor launches on which they should have made their escape were lying in the river, charred and burning wrecks. They had no alternative but to attempt an escape out of the dockyard area into the town and then out into the country. But, determined as his attempt was to get his remaining men out, it was in vain. He and many of his men were captured.

As Newman and his men were bundled into the German headquarters for interrogation, there was one thought uppermost in their minds—the *Campbeltown*. Would she blow up as planned or had the whole affair been a disastrous misadventure? They had until 10.30 am to wait for the answer.

The entire dockyard shook as almost five tons of explosives packed into the *Campbeltown* erupted in a deafening blast, blowing off the front third of the ship, knocking the caissons off the rollers and depositing them against the left-hand side of the dock. The water that gushed into the dock carried the *Campbeltown* with it and the wrecked ship ended up about halfway along the dock where it sank to the bottom.

Newman and his men leapt with joy. The raid was a success. The Normandie dock was out of action completely and it remained so until the end of the war. The whole point of the raid was to deny the mighty German battle-cruiser *Tirpitz* use of the dock and this had been done in one swift, sure blow. In fact she was never to reach the Atlantic as will be seen in another chapter.

To add further damage to the dock Lieutenant Wynn's two delayed action torpedoes blew up some days later throwing the Germans into a further panic.

Perhaps the most startling fact about the whole raid is that at no time before *Campbeltown* actually blew up did the Germans suspect that she was packed with explosives. In fact they made great play of the stupidity and the failure of the raid!

Of the entire force of motor launches which took part in the raid, only three returned home, having run the gaunlet of enemy fighters and bombers. Out of the 611 men who took part in the raid, 169 were killed, many were seriously wounded and many were prisoners. The other survivors were brought home onboard the destroyers *Tynedale* and *Arthurstone*.

The men who perished in that epic raid did not die in vain. But for their courage and sacrifice, *Tirpitz* might have put to sea and many hundreds of lives lost along with thousands of tons of shipping. The Second

World War could well have lasted much longer with a far more frightening result.

For their courage during and after the raid on St Nazaire, fifty-one men were Mentioned in Despatches, fifteen commandos were awarded the Military Medal, twenty-four sailors won the Distinguished Service Medal, five soldiers received the Distinguished Conduct Medal and four men won the Conspicuous Gallantry Medal. The Military Cross was awarded to eleven army officers, and seventeen naval officers were awarded the Distinguished Service Cross. Four officers were awarded the Distinguished Service Order.

The Victoria Cross, Britain's highest decoration for valour, was awarded to no less than five of the raiders, Lieutenant Colonel Newman, Commander Ryder, Lieutenant Commander Beattie, Able Seaman Savage and Sergeant Durrant, who became the first soldier ever to be awarded the VC in a naval action.

In the trying days of 1942, the courage of these men brought fresh hope of victory to the British nation and the Frenchmen who lived under the heel of the Nazi jackboot.

9

The Giant Killers

The Normandie dock at St Nazaire lay in ruins, wrecked by a determined band of soldiers and sailors, denying the German battle-cruiser *Tirpitz* her base in the Atlantic. But however certain the Admiralty was that *Tirpitz* would not make a break-out into the Atlantic no one could be absolutely positive that she might not take a chance. There was only one way of making certain that she never got the opportunity of playing havoc with Allied shipping and that was to sink her where she lay, in a Norwegian fiord.

Late in 1942, *Tirpitz* sailed from Bogenfiord to Trondheimfiord. The Admiralty decided that the time to attack her had come and the planners got to work. They agreed that the best form of attack would be by using two human torpedoes (or chariots) which would penetrate the extensive defences around *Tirpitz* then plant high explosives on or under the huge ship's hull. Alas, the mission was doomed to failure. While the two chariots were being towed by fishing boat into Trondheimfiord, their tow ropes were severed by the boat's propellers and both torpedoes were lost. But in spite of that setback the Royal Navy was determined to sink the *Tirpitz* and a new, and quite revolutionary type of craft was specially built for another attack on the German ship.

The navy's new secret weapon was the midget submarine, or X-craft as it was to be commonly known. It was essentially a miniature version of the big submarines, the difference being that instead of carrying torpedoes, it sported two detachable charges, each containing two tons of high explosives and it had no deck armament.

These mini-subs measured around forty-eight feet in length and had a maximum diameter of five-and-a-half feet, except under the periscope where it was possible for the ship's captain to stand upright, providing, of course, that he was of only average size. Weighing forty tons they were powered by diesel engines for surface cruising and batteries for underwater work. These batteries were housed in the forward compartment which also contained a store room, diver's breathing apparatus and suits. The compartment alongside that was known as the 'wet-and-dry' room and formed an escape chamber which allowed the divers to leave the craft and re-enter it while it was submerged.

The third compartment was the nerve centre and control room of the X-craft and was packed with a maze of complex control instruments. At the forward end of the compartment was the helmsman's position with the periscope housed in the middle. At the aft end sat the first lieutenant whose job was, amongst others, to operate the hydroplane controls. The fourth and last compartment housed the gyro compass, air compressor and a multitude of gauges, pipes and wheels, as well as the vital air conditioning plant.

The X-craft carried a crew of four comprised of the captain, first lieutenant, a third hand who served as the diver, and an Engine Room Artificer. Each man played a vital role and one of the most important was the diver whose job was, apart from attaching limpet mines to enemy craft, to cut a way through anti-submarine defence nets to allow the craft through and into the target area.

Once in the target area and alongside the enemy ship, the captain could either send the diver out to attach limpet mines to the ship's hull or simply detach the two two-ton charges and deposit them on the sea-bed underneath the ship's hull. With its job done the X-craft would make good its escape via its entry route.

That then was the secret weapon the navy had devised for their attack on *Tirpitz*, a mission fraught with danger and one made no easier for the crews by the uncomfortable and cramped conditions inside the X craft.

The operation was code-named 'Source' and its objective was to attack the capital ships moored in Altenfiord, yet another of the hundreds of Norwegian fiords into which *Tirpitz* had been moved as a further protective measure. She was joined there by two other warships, the *Lutzow* and *Scharnhorst*.

Six X-craft were to take part in the attack and they were each allocated their targets. Three were to attack *Tirpitz* itself. They were X5 (Lieutenant Henty-Creer RNVR), X6 (Lieutenant D. Cameron RNR) and X7 (Lieutenant B. Place RN). Two others, X9 (Sub-Lieutenant E. Kearon RNVR) and X10 (Lieutenant K. Hudspeth RANVR) were to attack *Scharnhorst* while the remaining craft, X8 (Lieutenant B. McFarlane RAN) was to attack *Lutzow*.

On 11 September 1943, these six craft left their depot ship HMS *Bonaventure* in Loch Cairnbawn in Scotland and began a perilous 1200-mile journey to Norway.

With the limited range of these craft and their slow speeds, they each had to be towed for the greater part of their journey by ocean-going submarines until they reached their 'slipping off' points near the entrance to Altenfiord where they parted company with the submarines. Alas, disaster struck long before they reached that point, when, in the tempestuous seas, X9 was lost with all hands.

The mission was to be dealt another blow when X8 had to be scuttled after developing mechanical faults. The attacking force had been whittled down to only four X-craft, three to attack *Tirpitz* and one to go for *Scharnhorst*.

Undeterred, the intrepid submariners pressed on, with the submarines ploughing through the sea like mother hens leading their chicks, until the time came for them to part from their parent subs. The X-craft crews bade their 'mothers' farewell and set course for the target—Altenfiord and the *Tirpitz*. There remained for them now the problem of escaping detection, penetrating minefields, slipping past an anti-submarine boom, cutting their way through *two* lots of anti-submarine nets, laying their charges under their targets then escaping through the same hazards yet again out to the open sea where they would rendezvous with their parent submarines. None of the men onboard these tiny craft was under any illusions about how difficult the task that lay ahead of him was to be.

But before they got within striking distance of their targets, misfortune was to strike them once more. X10 found that her target, the *Scharnhorst*, had left her moorings, and to make matters worse, the tiny craft was dogged with mechanical trouble. She had no choice but to abandon the operation and return to the open sea where she was taken in tow by the submarine *Stubborn*.

X5 disappeared without trace and the fate of the submarine and her crew is uncertain. Some authorities say that she was sighted by the *Tirpitz* outside the protective anti-submarine nets and sunk by the German ship's heavy guns but there is little positive evidence to substantiate this. Whatever her fate was, she was never seen again.

Only two X-craft now remained—X6, commanded by Lieutenant Cameron, and X7, whose captain was Lieutenant Place. Unaware of the fate that had befallen their comrades these two gallant commanders and their crews pressed on with their attack on *Tirpitz*. To get a clear picture of both their epic voyages up

Altenfiord and their subsequent attacks it is as well to trace each of them separately through to their conclusion.

Cameron, a quietly-spoken Scotsman, edged X6 into the forty-mile long Altenfiord under cover of darkness and began the hazardous voyage to the target. The submarine slid deeper into the fiord between the 3,000-foot-high cliffs which rose above it on either side while the crew could hear the tell-tale throb of engines on the surface as enemy boats scurried about their business. The tension became almost unbearable as X6 nosed nearer to its target, and to add to the difficulties the craft was dogged by mechanical trouble. The periscope, the very eyes of the submarine, became flooded and water seeped into one of the two-ton explosive charges, giving the boat a fifteen degree list. Dogged determination drove Cameron on through the minefield and anti-submarine boom until he was faced with the task of penetrating the two steel anti-submarine nets which surrounded the *Tirpitz*. As luck would have it, the nets were opened to allow a small German craft through and X6 slipped in. But her troubles were far from over. As Cameron manoeuvred her into attacking position the periscope became flooded again. Now Cameron was blind and the X-craft was floundering around in the fiord like a fish without eyes. Minutes later X6 crunched into an uncharted sandbank with her hull showing above the water.

A hawk-eyed lookout onboard *Tirpitz* reported seeing a 'big fish' in the water but amazingly he was told not to be a fool because there were no 'big fish' in the fiord—reason enough, one would think, for the Germans to investigate. Meanwhile, Cameron fought with the X-craft's controls and wriggled free of the bank, only to get caught up in the anti-submarine nets once more. This time there was no mistaking X6 for a big fish and a cry from *Tirpitz* brought German sailors rushing to the ship's rail with an assortment of weapons, machine-guns, rifles and small arms, to blaze away at the intruder. Luckily for Cameron, the big guns mounted on the German warship were incapable of shooting downwards, otherwise his boat would have been blasted clean out of the water.

As it was X6 was bombarded with machine-gun bullets which pinged off her metal casing until, with a resounding thud, she finally bumped into *Tirpitz*'s towering hull. While the barrage of fire continued, Cameron scraped his X-craft along the ship's side, releasing the two explosive charges as he went. Having shed his 'eggs', he realised that there was no chance of escape for him. The Germans would soon bring depth charges to bear on him as he fled from the target area and seal the fate of the mini-sub. He passed the word to the crew that he was going to scuttle the craft and he sent her to the bottom leaving himself and his three crewmen bobbing about in the water. Minutes later they were taken prisoner onboard *Tirpitz*—with four tons of their own high explosives lying beneath them.

Lieutenant Place's voyage to the target was no less eventful. His craft, X7, made her way into the fiord, dodging light craft as she went and she actually stopped at one point and surfaced to re-charge her batteries—right in the heart of the German's lair— then dived again. Then deeper into the fiord, Place rose to periscope depth to check his bearing and had to dive fast when he found himself in the path of a German launch which was pounding towards him. Amazingly, X7 was not spotted by the Germans and she slid farther up the fiord until Place reached the anti-submarine nets where the trouble began in earnest.

Place managed to negotiate the nets only to become entangled in the anti-torpedo nets. She was well and truly caught.

Place tried every move in the book to get free including flooding the inboard tanks in the hope that X7 would fall out of the nets with the increased weight but all his efforts were in vain. For an hour he struggled to get free until suddenly the boat got loose and shot to the surface. Hearts beat fast when the crew realised that they must be exposed to the enemy and they prayed that no look-out had spotted them. Place dived fast and lay doggo on the sea-bed until he reckoned it was safe to move once more. However he had still to penetrate the nets. He planned to go deep and slip underneath them but to his dismay, he hit the nets once more and again he had to struggle free. Once more he tried, this time at a greater depth and again he got entangled and eventually managed to wriggle free. When he got to the surface he saw to his amazement that he was on the other side of the nets and in a good position for his attack. How he did it will never be known. To this day, Place had no idea how he managed to get on the other side of the nets but however it had happened, he was there, and that was precisely where he wanted to be.

Place reckoned that he was almost thirty feet from *Tirpitz* and he set course for the attack. A few minutes later the X-craft slammed into the giant's side about twenty feet below the surface and slid along the hull while the charges were released. Then Place headed back in the direction he thought would bring him back to the spot where he had managed to get through the net but with no success. In fact he passed *under* the German ship several times trying every possible course in a bid to escape. But by then the Germans were dropping depth-charges into the water, trying desperately to sink the raider, but luck was with Place and the explosions did not harm the craft.

Moments later, Place surfaced and found himself half way across the *top* of the first net then his craft toppled over the side and dived towards the sea-bed. But it was not long before he was caught once again in a net and, as he fought to free the craft, his mind flashed to the clockwork fuses ticking away on the four tons of explosives he had planted under *Tirpitz*. Not long after, time ran out and the explosives erupted under *Tirpitz*, tossing X7 about and shaking her free of the nets but it did not, miraculously, seriously damage the X-craft's hull. But with depth-charges falling around them and the air supply running out fast the crew of X7 soon realised that there was no alternative but to abandon ship. Reluctantly, Place decided to surrender and try to save his crew so he surfaced slowly and waved a white sweater out of the conning tower. Immediately the firing stopped and Place scrambled out of the craft and on to the casing where he continued waving his 'flag' of surrender. But disaster was only seconds away. X7 hit a battle practice target and the sea poured in through the hatch before Place could shut it sending the sub plunging to the bottom of the fiord and leaving Place clinging to the practice target. Sadly, only Sub-Lieutenant Aitken succeeded in escaping from the stricken X-craft as it lay on the bottom and both he and Place were taken prisoner.

The damage done to *Tirpitz* was so serious that she was forced to remain at her anchorage for a further seven months before she was able to move to a new retreat at Tromsö. There, in November 1944, she was sunk by bombers of the Royal Air Force.

For their part in the *Tirpitz* raid Lieutenants Place and Cameron were both awarded the Victoria Cross. An extract from their citation read:

'. . . the courage, endurance, and utter contempt for danger in the immediate face of the enemy shown by Lieutenants Cameron and Place during this determined and successful attack were supreme . . .'

*   *   *   *

The success of 'Operation Source' spurred the Royal Navy on to further attacks in which the same courage, endurance and determination were ever present. The most dramatic of the missions which followed 'Source' was one which took place in an entirely different theatre of war—at the other side of the globe where the Royal Navy and her allies were doing battle with a fearsome enemy—the Imperial Japanese Navy.

The war in Europe ended in May 1945 when Germany surrendered unconditionally to the Allies but the fanatical Japanese continued fighting in the Far East.

In July 1945, the submarine depot ship HMS *Bonaventure* dropped anchor at Victoria harbour, Labuan, in the Far East. Onboard her were six XE-craft, ready to tackle the enemy in any way they could. These boats were improved versions of the ones which had attacked *Tirpitz* and were specially adapted for warfare in the hot climate of the Far East.

The XE-craft were put out to work immediately and several operations were carried out successfully but the most memorable and heroic was one in which XE1 and XE3 took part on 31 July.

It happened that at that time the 9,850-ton Japanese cruiser *Takao* and the cruiser *Myoko* were lying in the

Straits of Johore, the narrow strip of water between the island of Singapore and the mainland of Malaya.

The plan was that the two XE craft would be towed to a pre-arranged point then slipped-off. From there they would carry on independently, XE1 to attack the *Myoko* and XE3 to attack the *Takao*.

Lieutenant J. E. Smart (XE1) and Lieutenant Ian Fraser (XE3) studied the plan carefully and examined the charts of the strip of sea so that they knew exactly how they would go about their attack. Fraser's mission was perhaps the trickier of the two because the *Takao* was lying in very shallow water with depths ranging from only eleven to seventeen feet. She did, however, lie over a depression in the sea-bed with her bow and stern in water which at low tide dropped to less than three feet. Fraser decided that he would have to pass over the shallows and dive into the depression to place his explosives. With the depression only 500 feet across and 1500 feet long it did not give Fraser much room to manoeuvre his boat. He was convinced that the task set him was impossible but a minor thing like that did not deter him. His tiny XE-craft linked up with its parent submarine *Stygian* and, along with XE1 and her parent sub they put to sea.

So that the crews which were to make the attacks could do so fresh and alert, the craft were manned from their base to the 'slipping off' point by a 'passage crew'. Part of the job of this special crew was to ensure that each XE craft was passed over to the attack crew in perfect working condition and fighting order.

At 23.00 hours on the night of 30 July, the XE-craft changed hands and the attack crew took over then slipped their tow-ropes and set course towards their targets.

The captains and crews of both XE-craft were to

distinguish themselves that night but it is with the exploits of XE3, under the command of Lieutenant Ian Fraser, that we are concerned here, because for the men in that tiny submarine the attack was to be fraught with almost unbelievable danger.

Fraser stood on the boat's metal casing as he guided it on the surface through the first of the obstacles he was to meet that night—a minefield. Seemingly unperturbed, he navigated the craft through the mines that bobbed on the surface, held fast by their long anchor chains. One touch on the slender prongs which jutted out of these mines and the mission would be brought abruptly to a halt.

Black clouds hid the moon and made navigation difficult but Fraser continued to feel his way forward through the darkness until he approached a point where he knew the Japanese had positioned listening posts. He stopped engines and slid forward under battery power, every inch of the way waiting for the tell-tale boom of gun-fire that would signal their exposure. But luckily it did not come and once past the danger zone, Fraser started engines again and pressed on once more, altering position as best he could to take him on the right course for his target.

The tiny craft had not gone far when Fraser, still on the outer casing, caught sight of an object in the water some way away, which he thought was a buoy. He steered towards the object and to his horror discovered that it was no buoy but a fishing boat. He barked an order to ERA Reed, the helmsman, and XE3 swept away from the boat apparently unnoticed by the fishermen onboard.

The crew heaved a sigh of relief when the danger was past but an hour later they were to encounter more trouble. Fraser's eyes pierced the inky darkness and spotted two more ships approaching at speed and the craft dived quickly to avoid detection, remaining on the bottom until the throb of the enemy engines had disappeared.

On they went, with Fraser gingerly slipping deeper into the Johore Straits until the craft nosed through the defence boom which seemed to be kept permanently open.

At 00.50 hours Fraser sighted the *Takao* sitting motionless in the still water. The flat calm of the water made the attack even more difficult. If he were to make his run in with the periscope up, the trail left by the 'scope cutting through the water would betray his presence and without doubt spell disaster for him and his crew. He had no alternative but to rely only on quick periscope checks to get his bearings and set his course.

Ahead of XE3 sat the Japanese cruiser and tension mounted amongst the crew as Fraser closed in for the attack. Then he took one final glance through the periscope and his whole body chilled when he saw a Japanese launch crammed full of soldiers only yards away.

Perspiration poured off his brow. They were late for the attack and the tide was falling. There was no time to waste since he was fast running out of depth. But there was no turning back now and minutes later XE3 hit the *Takao* about the level of the bilge keel and far aft on the cruiser. Instantly the craft bounced down the cruiser's side and stuck in the mud.

Fraser wasn't satisfied that he was in the best position for the attack so he manoeuvred his craft out of the mud throwing great clouds of sand upwards as he did so and creating a terrible din. But by some fluke he was not detected.

Once free of the mud XE3 backed off again and Fraser took a peep through the periscope and lined up on the cruiser's forward funnel. Straining his eyes he could see the *Takao*'s hull looming up in front of him. Then in a few seconds there was blackness as the sub slid into the depression underneath the cruiser. She was perfectly positioned to drop her charges but the tide was falling quickly.

The cruiser was a mere foot above XE3's casing and Fraser allowed his crew to peer through the periscope at their target. But they had no time to linger. There was work to be done before the tide ebbed.

Fraser set about releasing his main charge which contained two tons of explosives but it would not budge. That form of attack was out for sure. His alternative was to attach limpet mines to the cruiser's hull and Leading Seaman Magennis, the XE-craft's frogman, was already pulling on his rubber suit and breathing apparatus. Magennis made his way into the wet-and-dry compartment, closed the connecting hatch and flooded the compartment but, when he tried to open the escape hatch, he found that he could not open it more then halfway—the lid was hard up against the bottom of the *Takao*. Undaunted, he removed his breathing apparatus and barely managed to squeeze out of the hatch, trailing his oxygen bottles behind him. Once outside he put his artificial lungs on once more—a feat that had never before been performed by a frogman in action.

Once outside, he set about the task of attaching the six limpet mines to the *Takao*'s hull which was a mass of razor-sharp shells, barnacles and seaweed. Magennis found that the limpets would not stick to the encrusted hull . . . the magnets used for attaching them would not hold on the surface so he set about chipping away the barnacles cutting his hands as he did so and tearing his rubber suit. At long last, after an agonising struggle with the barnacles, he succeeded in attaching the mines to the spots he had cleared with his diver's knife. The whole operation took half an hour before Magennis was able once more to squeeze back through the hatch with even greater difficulty than before.

Now that the diver was back inside the craft, Fraser set about releasing the port charge which contained the two tons of explosives. It slid away from the boat to rest on the sea-bed but when he tried to jettison the starboard limpet carrier, it would not budge. Try as he and the others might they could not move it. With the seconds racing by and the chances of detection growing greater every minute Fraser decided that it was time to go, with or without the limpet carrier.

Fraser ordered full astern and the engines groaned to pull the craft away—but nothing happened! XE3 was stuck fast. He tried moving the helm first in one direction then in the other in a bid to wriggle free but it was all to no avail. In a final, desperate bid to get free of the *Takao* before he and his crew were crushed to death, Fraser blew the main ballast tanks and the XE-craft shot backwards and rocketed to the surface breaking water only a few yards from yet another launch carrying Japanese troops. Immediately, Fraser dived again but still, after all their cavorting about underwater the limpet carrier would not free itself and the boat soon got out of control, doing nothing but travelling in circles.

There was no alternative but for one of the crew to don a frogman's suit and go out and prise the limpet carrier free. Fraser said he would go but Magennis wasn't having any of it. *He* was the diver and *he* would go. Once more, still exhausted and suffering from cut hands, Magennis entered the wet-and-dry compartment, this time armed with a huge spanner. Soon he was outside and thumping and hauling away at the offending piece of machinery. After fifteen minutes of gruelling work, the carrier at last slipped free and Magennis was able to return to the midget submarine. He was in such a state of exhaustion that he had to be pulled bodily from the wet-and-dry compartment.

With his job done, Fraser high-tailed it out of the Johore Straits and as he did so, there was an almighty explosion and the bottom was ripped out of the *Takao*. The mission was complete and XE3 met up with *Stygian* and was towed back to base where Fraser and his crew were given a hero's welcome.

Lieutenant Smart and XE1 had not been so lucky in their attack. He was delayed many times by enemy patrol-boat activity and forced to abandon his mission so he was determined that he was going to strike a blow at the Japs. Without knowing whether or not Fraser had laid his explosives, Smart took his craft alongside *Takao* and dropped his, then set course out of the danger area.

For their courage and daring in the attack on *Takao*, both Fraser and Magennis were awarded the Victoria Cross.

Bibliography

The War At Sea—Ed. John Winton (Hutchinson & Co.)

Eagle Fleet—W. E. Lucas (Weidenfeld & Nicolson.)

The Frogmen—T. J. Waldron & J. Gleeson (Evans Bros. Ltd.)

The Great War At Sea—A. A. Hoehling (Arthur Barker Ltd.)

Mein Weg Nach Scapa Flow—Günther Prien (Deutscher Verlag.)

Boys In Battle—John Laffin (Abelard-Schuman.)

The Smoke Screen of Jutland—Commander John Irving (William Kimber)

The Battle of the Atlantic—Donald Macintyre (B. T. Batsford Ltd.)

The German Navy in World War II—Edward P. Von Der Porten (Arthur Barker Ltd.)

Narvik—Donald Macintyre (Evans Bros. Ltd.)

Men of Glory—Macdonald Hastings (Hulton Press Ltd.)

More Men of Glory—Macdonald Hastings (Hulton Press Ltd.)

History of the First World War—Sir Basil Liddell-Hart (Cassell)

History of the Second World War—Sir Basil Liddell-Hart (Cassell)

Victoria Cross and George Cross (Imperial War Museum)

The Far And The Deep—Edward P. Stafford (Arthur
    Barker Ltd.)
Strike From The Sea—Robert Jackson (Arthur Barker
    Ltd.)
U-Boat—The Secret Menace—David Mason (Mac-
    donald)
Raid on St Nazaire—David Mason (Macdonald)
Aircraft and Sea Power—Vice Admiral Sir Arthur
    Hezlet (Peter Davies)
History of the Royal Navy—Peter Kemp (Arthur
    Barker Ltd.)